Salt on Our Lips

Stories of Humor, Humanity and Mysteries
Happily Unresolved

By Ken McAlpine

Ken McAlpine

Acknowledgments
Thank you to my friend Hank Tovar, who selflessly gives of his myriad talents. Thank you to Kay Giles, who has a better grasp on punctuation than I ever will. My friends bolster my faith in humanity.

Cover Photo Thailand Travel and Stock/Shutterstock

To my wife Kathy, who has been with me beside the water and made it magic.

INTRODUCTION

I need the sea because it teaches me
                    – Pablo Neruda

Once, on a honky-tonk beach boardwalk, a fortune teller called to me in his automated arcade voice, "Share with me thy bounty for my wisdom," but I saved my coins because the sea was behind me, and I already knew where to turn to find what I needed.

I have spent my life around the sea. I am not alone. Roughly 60% of the world's population lives in the coastal zone. No doubt, they each have their own reasons. One ocean lover proclaimed that nothing surpassed a night beach walk in winter. "You can see billions of stars and hear the waves roaring," he said. "It puts things in their place." The proprietor of a seaside pub told me, "I was driving a cab in Baltimore and somebody stuck a gun in the back of my head, and I was down here the next day watching the sunrise." Both seem like fine reasons to me.

There is one certainty.

The sea, it casts a spell. You do not recover.

The stories in this little book appear in rough chronological order, if for no other reason than convenience and the chance that, as time passed, I might have learned a few things along the way. They begin, in roundabout fashion, with birth ("Father"). A few stories are personal, but most were taken from an impossibly fortuitous career of being dispensed to various oceans and seaside haunts by magazine and book editors. Even as I write this, so much luck looks like a lie.

If you have made your own life around the sea, you know it is a place of profound beauty and undefinable mystery. The beauty, you have enjoyed. The mystery, you don't have to define. A child chases seagulls by the water's edge, even though the cause is hopeless, for the joy of the chase and the hint of faint possibility. I wrote these stories for the same reason. Putting the sea, and her (how can something so tempestuous and bewitching be anything but a woman?) myriad moments and subtle lessons, into precisely the right words is impossible. But I have loved the chase.

Sun-baked salt pinching the skin, dune grass silvered by moonlight, sea breezes whispering like lovers' sighs, possibly accompanying lovers' sighs. Close your eyes and conjure your own memories from the lullaby tumblings of the sea.

Someone once told me, "Water separates the foul from the pure." I like that.

Make no mistake, the sea is also a dark and harsh place that cares nothing for us. Walking the shoreline of Cape Cod, cocooned in wind and wave, Henry David Thoreau happened upon an old man sitting on the sand. Thoreau assumed the old man was also enjoying the sea's symphony, and remarked as much in a neighborly manner. The man barked back that he did not enjoy the sea at all: his son had been lost at sea in a storm. On Oakland Beach, in Narragansett Bay, I heard the story of a deadly hurricane that roared ashore in the fall of 1938. As the winds rose to a shrieking siren, a man sat on the beach and waited. Friends frantically urged him to leave, but he refused. His son had drowned six years earlier. "He's come for me," the man said. "My boy has come for me at last." One story of terrible loss rests in these pages. I have left out the names, but this man knows who he is, and should he ever read this book, I apologize deeply if reading his story causes him pain again.

But even in darkness, light resides. At least one lesson bestowed by the sea is clear. Live life now. Commercial fishing is one of the most dangerous occupations you'll find. If you ever want to have the time of your life (and possibly walk the razor's edge of legality), spend time with commercial fishermen. You won't be sorry. The sea demands a degree of foolish childishness, and there are plenty of children of the sea. I am proud to stand among them. "Breathe deeply and live wildly," someone once said. I don't know who it was, but I'd bet they were educated by the sea.

The sea molds special folk, and it has been my privilege and joy to make acquaintance with more than my share of them. I have learned from each and every one. Some appear in these pages. Some were worldly and nearly oracle-wise. Some were insular and, depending on how you judge such things, perhaps ignorant. A fisherman from Montauk, Long Island got a raucous laugh out of telling me how he had once informed a fisherman friend that he would be traveling to

Spain. "Oh," was the reply. "Are you driving there?" I knew, without him telling me, that at that moment, his friend was sitting on the bar stool beside him, for he laughed just as hard, and didn't give a rat's ass about impressing me or anyone else. How can you not be made better by crossing paths with such folk?

But folk pass and the sea remains, casting its spell on a new generation. When our sons were very young, we stood together on a beach. The youngest asked, "Does the water keep going on?" Yes. And therein lies the beauty.

My beautiful bride and I raised our two sons beside the sea, and now the same happy disease rests inside them. I had my faults as a father, but it makes me happy to know our sons are now forever bewitched. Now they will strive for a lifetime to chase down the mystery, watching as it rises casually out of reach again and again. So be it. But they will also know the sheer foolish joy and, if they pay close attention, just as they once pocketed shells, they might also gather a pocketful of truths. When my time as a father and husband is complete, I hope my sons will scatter my ashes across the water and share a good laugh.

Until then, I will continue to thrill to the chase.

Thanks for joining me.

Sincerely, Ken McAlpine
Ventura, California
October 2015

FATHER

My father went bodysurfing the day before I was born: he wanted to go the day I was born too. He and my mother were living in Hong Kong, where my father worked as a diplomat for the United States Embassy. My father is a quiet man who specializes in stable, common sense decisions, but he has his weak moments. Had it not been for my mother, who wisely decided they should visit the hospital instead, I would have been born on the sands of Tai Long Wan, known locally as Big Wave Bay, my mother shouting for my father's head while my father's head bobbed merrily among the waves.

My father still loves to bodysurf, and as soon as I knew how to swim, he taught me. I suppose he kept an eye on me in those first days: along with being sensible and stable, my father is annoyingly responsible. But part of me wonders. I have since come to see that my father bodysurfs, for the most part, with his face planted in the water, lifting his head only to grin or breathe. It's as if he's shutting out the rest of the world, or maybe he does it so he can ride the wave until the tip of his nose scrapes the sandy bottom. When my father plunged into the ocean, he became a different man. He'd ride waves for hours. After each ride he'd stand up in the inches of water in which he found himself, and hitch up his suit, for he was a thin man and frugal too: the mopey waistline of his threadbare suit was no match for his nearly nonexistent hips. Assured he would not be arrested for bare-bottomed impropriety, my quiet, stable father would high step back out through the incoming waves as if he were four and the gates to Disneyland were closing out at sea.

He taught me to bodysurf, and for a time, though he would never tell me so, I'm sure our communal wave riding provided him joy. I've seen the grainy snapshots my mother took, the two of us riding the same wave, grinning the same slap happy grin.

Eventually, however, his introduction blew up in his face. A child's role is to break away, and when I was sixteen, I discovered surfing. We still vacationed each summer in the small town of Bethany Beach, Delaware, but I was beyond that now. The anemic waves a short walk from our rented cottage weren't enough. I borrowed a surfboard. Each morning at dawn I'd wedge the board into the back of our family station wagon, my father would hand me the keys, and I'd make the short drive to Ocean City, Maryland, where I'd ride equally anemic waves.

When I'd return to our weathered beach cottage, the station wagon ticking in the loamy drive, my father, who well understood the dynamics of surf on a ruler-straight coastline, would ask me how the waves were, and I would lie and he would smile, telling me that was great. I'd bodysurf a few waves with him, but not many. I was living for the next morning. I had moved beyond him, devoted to something he couldn't understand. Two strokes, a moment's weightlessness, and you went missing from the world.

I fell in love with the ocean and surfing, loving them, without exception, above all else. After my first year of college, I took a summer job as an ocean lifeguard in Ocean City, New Jersey. At first my father accepted this. I suspect he even liked it. It gave him the excuse to come up from their landlocked Virginia home to bodysurf. Lifeguarding was an acceptable job for a young man still studying for a career. But then I graduated from college, and I kept doing it. I worked the beaches of Ocean City in the summer, went down to Fort Lauderdale, Florida and guarded there in the winter, and then returned to Jersey's beaches when summer rolled around again. I surfed anywhere and everywhere. I owned three surfboards and, if I searched hard enough, one pair of shoes. My hair was brittle, and my lips always tasted of salt. It was all I ever wanted.

Once my father visited me in Fort Lauderdale, where I lived with six other lifeguards who behaved themselves the night my father came to our house. Not so our next door neighbor, also our landlord, who was entertaining a vocal member of the opposite sex. When their activities reached a crescendo, their screams rang through his house and ours.

My father sipped his lemonade.

"I hope he's not collecting the rent."

The next summer, visiting me on the beach in Ocean City, my father spied an older guard. My father has always had a sixth sense for the things that make me squirm, and so he turned to me and asked where Eric was going to school. Only on rare occasions have I been able to lie to my father, and this was not one of them. Eric, I said, had graduated from law school two years earlier.

"My," said my father. "He's done well."

It wasn't a poke at Eric. We both knew that.

I did Eric several better. Graduating from college, I dispensed with the façade of graduate education entirely. I guarded for a winter in Fort Lauderdale and returned to Ocean City for the summer. The next winter I worked as a lifeguard at the health club swimming pool at Resorts International Casino in Atlantic City. Suffice to say this was not a taxing job, mentally or physically, though once I did have to summon just the right words, politely informing one of the casino's highest rollers that losing his shorts at blackjack didn't provide him the right to swim without them in a public pool. There was a gunslinger's moment of standoff – him considering having me fired or placed in cement boot; me wondering where I would find another lifeguarding job in New Jersey in December – and then he smiled at me and said, "You've got balls." Then he asked for a towel, and when I handed it to him, he gave me a twenty dollar bill, and I wondered if I should have gone into diplomacy like my father.

For several years I made my way in the world as a lifeguard, a pot scrubber and a landscaper – a career track that led nowhere except the ocean's edge, which was precisely where I wanted to be. I surfed in Bali. I drove up the east coast of Australia, surfing, camping on empty beaches and engaging in intellectually stimulating conversations, most often in pubs.

My new best friend, waving vaguely in the direction of a sign hanging upside down behind the bar: "Whattayer think of *that*?"

Me, squinting: "It's too dark to read it."

Him: "It's bloody noon, you wanker!"

Me, squinting harder:
"If…you…drink…then…drive…you're…a… bloody…idiot."

Him: "Pig's arse! At last we know who we are!"

Not that I wasn't getting an education. One night, for reasons unclear to me, I fell asleep in a local cemetery. The following morning, leaving as quickly and respectfully as I could, I noticed one of the headstones. *There Is No Cure For Birth and Death Save to Enjoy the Interval.*

It was just the confirmation I needed.

My father did not agree. He hated the path I had chosen. It aggravated him, just as he aggravated me. He was everything I was not. Dependable, responsible, organized, financially successful. He had neat rows of suits in his closet. I once financed a week of meals using the change on the floor of my car. When we saw each other the air hummed, and soon enough, short-circuited. I was ruining my life. My father told me this dozens of times, hundreds of times, I don't know how many times, because I only remember one. Done with his lecture about opportunity passing me by, he gazed off to some horizon only he could see.

"Sometimes," he said softly, "I wish I'd done what you've done."

Not long ago I visited Big Wave Bay. I was on an assignment, writing a magazine story on Hong Kong. I walked across the sand, bright under my feet, until I stood at the ocean's edge. The waves were small – no Big Wave Bay today – but they looked fun. I watched them for a long time, and then I left. I had shoes on, and an afternoon appointment.

When I returned to California I called my father. He is no longer a young father. Neither am I. I told him where I had stood.

There was quiet on the line. No one can say for certain what another human being is thinking, and I didn't ask my father: he is too private for that. But I'm pretty sure I know where he was.

In the quiet we looked out over the water we shared.

BE STUPID

When I was nineteen, my friend Dennis and I drove to the Outer Banks of North Carolina for Thanksgiving. We were in college at the University of Virginia. We had a few days off from school. We drove past gray cities, then slow-moving towns, and finally farms, ice-glazed and still. We drove across the wind-whipped Pamlico Sound. The Sound leapt and churned, the water the color of chocolate milk.

We spent our first hour on the Outer Banks looking for the cheapest motel we could find. We found it in Nags Head. We stood at the front counter. The desk clerk looked out the frosted windows to where snow flurries now danced. His eyes took in our car.

"I hope you have the right gear," he said.

"We do," I said, and it was only half a lie.

"If you don't, you'd be stupid to go," he said.

We paid with a fistful of wrinkled bills. We had a little left for gas, a little for beer, and a little less for food. Food didn't matter. We had a whole cooked turkey in the cooler we brought into the room. Dennis had cooked the turkey back at the house we shared with two other friends. Dennis loved to cook, and he was good at it. Mostly, he improvised. He would rummage through the cabinets, using whatever ingredients struck his fancy, making things up as he went along. He combined ingredients that would raise the hairs on the back of a real chef's neck. He would shake in a little of this and a lot of that. If he used a cookbook, I never saw it. I don't know what he used to season this particular turkey, but whatever it was, it was just right: the entire drive down, otherworldly smells tormented us.

The minute we got in the room, we opened the cooler and pulled out the turkey. Honeymooners don't get down to business faster. Dennis had remembered to bring a platter for the turkey, but I had forgotten the silverware. It didn't matter. Dennis had outdone himself. In short order everything, including us, smelled of turkey. Outside the wind roared and the snow cavorted in schizophrenic circles. In the motel room the heater clattered, and drafts pushed through the walls, nudging greasy paper towels.

The motel was on the beach. Our room faced east. Over the tops of the dunes, we could see the white-capped ocean.

Dennis rarely hesitated. He didn't hesitate now.

"Let's go," he said.

We pulled on our wetsuits. Outside, the snow bit at our faces. It took us longer than it should have to get the surfboards off the car racks. Our fingers were already half frozen.

A wooden walkway crossed the dunes. The snow made a light dusting on the wood. Dennis walked in front of me. To this day I can still see the enormous prints of his bare feet. My own feet ached as much as my hands. Plenty of people surf in the winter, but they are generally prepared, covered from head to toe – neoprene hood for the head, neoprene boots and gloves for the feet and hands - in wetsuit. I had lied to the desk clerk. We had brought what we had.

By the time we stepped on to the frozen beach everything ached and stung, but I didn't feel right about whining. I had no hood, boots or gloves, but at least my wetsuit extended all the way to my ankles. Dennis's wetsuit reached only to his knees. His calves had turned a curious red.

Snow had gathered in Dennis's hair. I knew what he would look like when he got old.

On the exposed beach, the wind roared even louder. It sounded a bit like laughter. Brown gobbets of foam quivered on the sand.

Dennis stopped. He looked at the ocean, gray and heaving, and then he looked to me because there was no one else to consult.

"What's the water temperature?" he asked.

"Forty-six."

"Are we stupid?"

"Yes," I said.

Dennis watched me for another long moment.

"I hope we have enough turkey," he said, and then he walked into the ocean.

I can't recall how long we stayed in the water, but it probably wasn't more than ten minutes. The waves were angry and roared in from every direction, clobbering us and punching the breath from our lungs and spinning us underwater in an oddly serene darkness. But we were nineteen, and Dennis was an All-American swimmer with lungs like a Hoover vacuum, and we were both so in love with the thrill of riding a wave that all the clobbering was worth it. You see, I had only half lied to the desk clerk. The right gear isn't just something you buy.

I don't remember how many waves we caught, but it was certainly less than we could count on one hand, and then we were running up the beach, half laughing and half weeping, partly because we were deathly cold, partly because Dennis jolted up the beach like a man on stilts, his legs now a nauseating shade of purple. Everything burned, and we were alive.

We surfed again the next day.

As I write this it seems like yesterday, but it isn't. My friend Dennis died yesterday. His lungs killed him. That's where the cancer started.

It's stupid not to do the things you can.

SUMMER LOVE

Summer love is breathtakingly unfathomable, but it tastes like salt. It feels like a still attic room, white linen curtains hanging limp. It sounds of sighs and sea breezes. It smells intimate. Two, lost in the musky heat of being alive.

And after, salt drying on your skin.

Summer's shore is made for love. Heat. Skin. Instinct. Enchantment. Suns like balm. Moons like promise. A pressure cooker of wanton energy. Everyone – young, middle-aged and old – feels the humming undercurrent, the electricity of a perpetual sensual storm. No, summer love doesn't belong solely to the young, but they are the ones who make a symphony of it. If you are past young, you know this. If you are young now, you will know this later, but now you are preoccupied. Nights that drift into dawns. Innocence fumbling toward discovery. Night moves, Bob Seger called them, but they are as ably performed in those still attic rooms, where the heat of midday joins the heat of movement. In most instances summer love is closer to lust, but lust is a form of love meant to be enjoyed. Summer love, like lust, has no distractions. No past. In most cases, no future. There is only the immediate now, and when distant tomorrow arrives, more moments of now. Summer is all. Fall is a distant shadow unseen, and when it comes it will leave first heartache, and then memories. Because everything ends. But the young don't think that way, and there is simplicity and profound beauty in this.

Summer love unfolds on every shore. Mine was Ocean City, New Jersey, which, if you know straightforward New Jersey, is known, rightly, as The Shore. I spent eight summers in Ocean City, from Memorial Day until Labor Day's poignant farewell, and, thirty years later, I cannot rid myself of the place. Just thinking about those summers makes my chest tighten, as if, for a brief moment, it has forgotten the mechanics of breathing. The summer loves I had there are indelible. I am forever ruined, and it is wonderful.

Since those summers, I have returned to Ocean City now and again. Things have changed, but mostly the town remains the same, an old-fashioned slice of summertime Americana, a place unapologetically staid and square, where sunburned families still play Crazy Eights around the kitchen table at night, and Ferris wheels chew slowly through the salty air and, on boardwalk benches facing the sea, old couples inhale the smell of creosote and cotton candy and stare out to the Atlantic and memories only they can see. It is possible they keep those memories to themselves.

I remember bright eyes of blue, and dark eyes of caution and then acceptance, and green eyes of trust. I remember first kisses. I remember taut limbs and satin skin and smooth curves: tan skin flowing to white, and sweat beaded on downy upper lips. I remember empty dunes cloaked in nightshade and, behind locked doors (because I always lived with a Mongol horde of roommates: not a descriptor chosen randomly), attic rooms bright with pleasure and sunlight. I remember the precise contents of night picnics (Combo pretzels, apple slices, cheese, wine, many candles and one blanket). I remember parties, bars, and more parties, for alcohol performed unlockings. I remember dinners cooked together, then eaten hurriedly: the mess cleaned up (maybe) the next morning. I remember Ferris wheel rides, Atlantic City's casinos winking in the distance – fate, chance, fate, chance -- two sun-burnished faces penny-bright in the Ferris wheel's garish lights. I still feel the spring of boardwalk beneath my feet: hear the whisper of cotton as a summer dress danced in a nighttime ocean breeze. I still feel the heat of being alive.

I cup these memories as delicately as a child holds a butterfly. Just as, sometimes late at night, I now listen to my wife's soft breaths, knowing that this moment, too, is already gone.

Love comes in many forms and at any time, but for me the love that mattered came in summer, and that has made all the difference. This girl was different. I'd be lying if I said I knew it at that moment, the two of us, at the end of a first date, sitting on a night jetty in sudden awkward silence, staring at waves flashing white in the dark. Mist tumbled in. The world smelled of salt and perfume and my hands shook, and I did something strange. Until that moment, kisses were unspoken. This time I asked for permission. I asked with a strange seriousness, a formality stiff as a cinderblock. In romance novels, men boldly take the initiative. They don't stutter and crush their fingers and hold their breath in the face of their indecisiveness. I did all of these things. And this girl looked into my baffled, terrified face and smiled without a stutter and said yes.

Mist kept tumbling in. I tasted salt on both our lips.

Some years later, beside another shore, I sat at a restaurant with this girl, now a beautiful young woman and my wife. We had spent the day on the beach. The sun's burnish always brings out the green in her trusting eyes. Her face was radiant. She consulted the menu, but she kept glancing up at me because, I confess, I stared. I should have been studying the menu because there were many things I couldn't pronounce and, being a fine restaurant, there weren't numbers beside the entrees.

My wife smiled. If you are very lucky, summer's love transcends lust and sweet naiveté and becomes something deeper and sweeter, so that sometimes your lover knows exactly what you are thinking.

"You know, you *could* order from the children's menu," she said.

Green eyes watched me, then lifted to look over my shoulder.

"I ordered an appetizer," she said. "I hope you don't mind."

I could not recall her ordering, but it was also true I had been staring. I noticed now how her hands fidgeted. The waiter came up behind me. My wife's hands dropped to smooth the napkin in her lap, but her eyes were now locked on mine.

It was a small silver platter, but it was more than big enough. A pair of booties rested on the platter, each no bigger than a thumb. Such tiny feet: it seemed impossible.

I stared at my wife, but hard as I tried, I couldn't see her clearly.

I tasted salt on my lips.

Memories sweet and simple as soft ice cream, and as breathtakingly unfathomable as summer love. You may know them. Or, if you are young, perhaps your chance waits in the green-blue-dark eyes of a no-longer-stranger. Summer's power and magic is her timelessness. Breathtaking history repeats itself along the wave-tossed shore.

Our summer love has gone to fall. One day, if we are lucky, it will proceed to winter.

But we will always feel summer's heat.

CRABBING

Tucked within the protected confines of Nantucket Sound, Quohog Beach is a beach for children. As if attempting to make things pleasant for its primary patrons, everything about Quohog Beach is small, from its wee crescent of sand to the pint-size jetty jutting like a blunt thumb into Nantucket Sound.

For the moment we are consumed with the beach. Buckets swinging in our hands, we scour the sand, poking through tangles of seaweed, broken bits of whelk and moon snail, searching beneath a cloudless blue July sky for pieces of horseshoe crab. These prehistoric creatures once littered Cape Cod in such numbers that they were ground up and used as fertilizer by farmers. From what we observe upon Quohog Beach, their numbers haven't decreased much, though each crab appears to have been placed atop a firecracker and then scattered by a schizophrenic wind.

No matter. Our plan remains straightforward. We will piece together a horseshoe crab, whole and perfectly complete. Cullen and Graham raptly pluck cracker-thin crab bits, placing them gently in their buckets. I follow their example, but with slightly less enthusiasm. I understand the odds. I glance at other parents, flat on their backs in the hot sun.

At six, Cullen runs things. He waves a magisterial hand at his four-year-old brother.

"If we don't get enough pieces to put together the crab now," he decrees, "we'll get the rest later."

"Uh-huh," grunts Graham, possibly because he mildly resents being bossed around, possibly because he is sorely bent to one side under the weight of a bucket spilling over with pretty much everything he could pick up.

Cullen strides over to his brother's bucket, peers in and scowls.

"Crabs aren't made out of beer cans!"

I wish the beer can was full. My head has been cocked to the sand for two hours. The back of my neck feels like it's been kicked by a Clydesdale.

Perhaps I slip into sudsy daydream. Cullen looks at us both and harrumphs.

"Am I going to have to do this all by myself?"

We collect jigsaw pieces for another thirty minutes. Not thirty-one minutes, not thirty-two. Any parent of small children understands exactitude. I can't go a minute longer. I find an excuse called lunch.

The three of us walk up the path to the cottage where we are staying for the week, buckets bumping.

"I think we have the pieces we need," says Cullen.

"Right," says Graham.

He is too young for sarcasm.

We march through the front door and continue, as quickly as possible, on through the kitchen, where Kathy is fixing everyone lunch. We are not quick enough.

"You'd better wash whatever that is off their hands," says Kathy.

I stand in the bathroom, watching Cullen turn a white hand towel black. I may be less attentive the second son around. As we eat lunch I notice Graham has something shiny and snail-like on his index finger. I say a silent prayer and he answers it by licking it off.

That night Kathy and I lay in bed. The sliding screen door opens to the porch. Occasionally a puff of wind brings a smell that makes me wonder if Stephen King is cooking something just outside. Beneath the stars dark shells lay methodically sorted, according to what, I don't know.

"Phew," I say.

"Maybe you could put them in the yard," Kathy says, but I know she doesn't really mean it because she's smiling as if we're laying downwind from a potpourri factory.

"Don't worry," I say. "Another six months and it'll be a wrap."

"Anything is possible," my beautiful bride says to me, and I know why I married her.

The following morning we redirect slightly.

"I want to crab," says Graham.

Cullen gives a magisterial nod.

"Let's," he says.

We have become fascinated with crabbing because frankly nothing, with the possible exception of King Henry VIII, eats with more gusto than crabs do. Also, live crabs do more interesting things than dead ones. The small jetty pronging off Quohog Beach is loaded with crabs. We know this because on this, the fourth day of our vacation, we have already been crabbing roughly two thousand times.

We retrieve our buckets from the porch. Before we go, Cullen crouches to arrange a few promising horseshoe pieces.

"Hmmm," he says, moving the pieces in circles like a centrifugal chess master.

"Hmmm," says Graham, who at this juncture in time still admires his older brother greatly.

Cullen finishes placing the bits in their proper places. There is something resembling a horseshoe crab body, but there are still great gaps occupied by cedar composite decking.

"There," says Cullen.

What I see resembles a horse dropping after the Kentucky Derby field has run through it.

Cullen looks to Graham.

"Just a few more pieces," he says.

"Hmmmm," says Graham.

Small children wake well before the most conscientious rooster, and even earlier on vacation. The world is gray. The light isn't even up yet. The air is damp with sea. The beach is empty.

We each carry our own bucket, chicken bits and string inside. I step gingerly along the jetty. The enormous rocks, sectioned in some distant quarry, are liberally colonized by barnacles that stab at the soles of my feet.

Cullen and Graham walk as if strolling across shag carpet. When I reach the end of the jetty Cullen is already crouched, peering into his chosen crevice.

"Breakfast time," says Cullen, "but not for us."

Graham is flat on his stomach, his face and the majority of his torso in his crevice of choice.

"What do you see?" I ask.

"I dropped my string."

After I retrieve it, I tie a chicken piece to each string. The boys accept their strings, solemnly lowering the sacrificial chicken into the dark rift. I spread out the newspaper I brought, and put the remaining chicken pieces on it. Past experience has shown us we'll quickly need room in our buckets for crabs.

When I finish said preparations, I squat and watch our sons. They peer down into the dark, brows furrowed.

"Come awwwwwwwn," says Cullen.

Graham's string jerks.

"Whaaaaaat!" he shrieks. "Caught one! Caught one!"

I have coached them thoroughly in the craft of crabbing. Wait for the crab to latch firmly to the chicken. Bring the string up slowly so the crab doesn't know it's being reeled in.

Graham stands straight up, flinging his hands in the hair. The crab performs a lazy parabolic arc through the air, then settles to swing to and fro in front of Graham's belly button, a dark pendulum oblivious to its change in circumstance. One claw affixed to the chicken bit, the other claw greedily spoons meat into its wet maw.

Reaching behind the crab, I pinch its body between my thumb and forefinger and pry it, with considerable force, from the now shredded chicken wing. I put it in Graham's bucket where it makes a mad scrabbling.

"I was careful," says Graham proudly.

Cullen pretends to ignore all this. His string is limp.

"I caught a crab," says Graham, who is not yet schooled in subterfuge either.

"*You* pick up beer cans," says Cullen.

Just when I start believing that the crabs in Cullen's crevice have evolved into something wiser, they start leaping at his string as if they've suddenly realized they're aboard the Titanic. They rise from their dark places furiously stuffing down chicken bits, exhibiting not a whiff of self-preservation.

There's always opportunity for imparting parental wisdom.

"Crabs are called crustaceans," I say. "Even though their shells are hard, you still need to be really careful. If you break off their claws, they won't be able to eat."

"If their claw breaks off, a new one grows on," says Cullen.

"It does?"

"I dropped my string," says Graham.

The crabs now pour from the jetty like a locust horde, striking wantonly at the chicken bits and each other with harsh clicks. There is a parable here, the downfall wrought by selfishness and greed, but the boys are too young for that. Crabs are also distantly related to insects, but I keep this to myself too because I'm afraid Cullen will correct me.

In short order all three buckets are brimming with clacking crabs.

"We need to empty the buckets," I say.

"I'll do it," says Cullen.

"Pour them out in the water," I tell him. "You don't want them cracking their shells on the rocks. Climb down the side of the jetty. You'll have to lean out a little. Take one bucket at a time, and be careful."

Perhaps I should be reported to Childhood Protective Services, but the water here is only a few feet deep and I want our boys to stretch.

Cullen inches carefully down the side of the jetty feet first, crab-like himself. When they are young, they follow your directions to the letter. He settles easily on a broad rock washed with a thin skein of surge. The spilling crabs make a sound like a fistful of rocks flung into the water.

I know what to look for next. I grab Graham before he can slide down.

"Your job is to get the buckets when Cullen passes them up," I say.

His solemn nod assures me this is responsibility enough. But something in his eyes tells me he's solemn for a different reason.

He looks toward the beach.

"We're not going to find enough horseshoe crab pieces," he says.

"We might," I say.

"Maybe not," he says.

I want them to believe anything is possible, but I want them to prepare for disappointment too.

"We might not find enough pieces," I say, and I feel something stick in my throat.

We return to crabbing. Cullen stays where he is, but Graham wordlessly moves close to me, sharing my crevice. It is quiet. I hear his small breaths. I feel the butterfly press of his hand on my thigh.

The sun breaks through the dawn clouds, striking the water with silver shafts. Together we breathe.

Sometimes life's pieces fit together in ways you don't expect.

DAVID

Kayaking off Ocracoke Island, North Carolina, I met a man named David. It was Thanksgiving and brutally cold, a hard, damp wind producing an uncountable army of whitecaps on Pamlico Sound. When I met David, he was bobbing at the mouth of Ocracoke's tiny harbor. I saw him before he saw me. His head was down, consulting the navigational chart spread across the deck of his kayak. He had a compass too.

It is bad form to paddle silently past the only other kayaker for miles.

"Beautiful out here, isn't it?" I said.

It was, in a frozen, gray, victory-at-sea fashion.

David's head came up slowly, as if reluctant to leave the chart. He appeared to be in his fifties, though it was hard to tell, as only a small portion of his face emerged from the bubble-wrap of protective gear. I was wearing nothing but a wetsuit, and perhaps a bluish complexion. As for navigation, well I knew north from south.

David looked at me like the idiot I was.

"It's a little cold," he said. "Where are you heading?"

"I don't know," I said.

This was largely true. I knew I was turning left once I exited the harbor, but now, in the face of this man's foresight, this didn't seem a very proud plan.

"Ah," said David.

We bobbed on the water, the wind beating between us, and exchanged pleasantries. David had come to Ocracoke for the long Thanksgiving weekend.

He didn't smile as we talked, but his tone was amiable. I had drifted close enough to see that he had a small plastic orb affixed to the shoulder of his jacket. Technologically speaking, it resembled one of those Christmas snow globes, only instead of swirling snowflakes, it contained a winking light.

His eyes followed mine.

"GPS," he said. "I'm one of those people who like to plan."

David asked where I was from, and when I told him California, he said his wife's family lived in California.

"My wife died about a year and a half ago," he said. "Of cancer."

The wind whistled. The afternoon turned colder.

"You know, she loved to kayak," he said to me. "She really wanted to come here, but we just kept putting it off."

The whitecaps bumped us.

It's impossible to find the right words for sorrow like this. So I said what I felt, and the words seemed pointless and trite: "I'm so sorry."

Then I realized David was finishing his voyage, not beginning it.

"I was just paddling in a sluice back there," David continued, more to himself than me. "There were herons and egrets. It probably goes back two miles. I was paddling back there and I'm thinking, 'This is one of the most beautiful places I've ever seen.'"

I paddled to David's sluice. Sheltered from the wind, the sluice, little wider than my paddle in most places, snaked into the interior of the island, through straw-colored marsh grass and a few guano-stained trees. The water was less than a foot deep in some places. The tide was running out, and beneath the water's smooth, gin-clear surface I could see tiny bird tracks across the mud bottom, fine, graceful etchings that sang of flight.

I floated on the mirror surface to the whisper of marsh grass. Out of the wind it was warm. Birds sang, and egrets, snow-white and silent, swooped low, dropping below the grass line to their own secrets.

When I finally turned around, I stopped paddling and closed my eyes, and the tide's delicate tug drew me slowly back to the Sound.

It was lovely, but it was hung with sadness, too, this beautiful place given to me by a man who couldn't plan for everything.

EYES WIDE OPEN

There is a place off the South Shore of Kauai, within sight of the condos and high rises of Poipu, where prehistoric miracles reside. The underwater caverns are not deep, maybe thirty feet. They are tidy and compact, a sort of oceanic Hobbit hole, and most times (for nothing about the ocean is predictable) Sheraton Caverns are jammed with an impressive assemblage of green sea turtles.

On this squinty-bright morning, green sea turtles (and a smattering of hawksbills) are everywhere. They fill the waters surrounding the caverns, swimming with balletic grace, changing direction with the slightest flipper dip, as if they have done this for 220 million years. Their hummocked backs are scarred, dark and mossy, but the sunlight plays off their smooth, creamy- plated undersides (known as the plastron, should you ever find yourself short on cocktail conversation) in hypnotic ripples.

Within the caverns – lava tubes, actually – additional turtles lay on rock shelves. Some stare out at the visiting divers: a sea turtle can do many astonishing things, but it cannot retract its head into its shell. Perhaps to compensate, many turtles are jammed into their rock shelf slots head first, like landings gone awry. My fellow divers snap pictures of their prehistoric rumps. I do not take photos, for I am disorganized, and even losing a cheap underwater camera is a sore blow, but I swim very slowly, snapping photos with my mind's eye. The slower I fin, the more turtles I see. Everywhere, humped shadows lodge in dark recesses. It's the reptilian version of a Paris youth hostel.

There is nowhere else I would rather be, and so, as my fellow divers leave the caverns one by one to see what they might encounter in the open water, inside the caverns I drop to my elbows and knees in the sand. Perhaps I look like a rock, more likely the turtles don't care a cuss for me, but as I lay in the sand, an arm's length away three turtles perform the loveliest choreography, circling and weaving about each other like somnolent acrobats. Eternal dusk reigns within the caverns, perfect light for these prehistoric pirouettes. In this sepia world, it is not hard to imagine different seas beyond the caverns, seas filled not with sunburnt tourists, but with creatures of otherworldly dimension and adaptation, crushing jaws lined with scythe teeth, predators who come upon their prey as silent arrows on a soundless wind. Seas beyond Kauai's time. At six million years of age, Kauai is the oldest of the main Hawaiian Islands. Her residency is laughable compared with that of the creatures I watch now.

With a cloudy puff, I lift off the sand and follow a large turtle toward the surface. This turtle, too, cares nothing for my presence. We rise together, scaly flippers inches from pimply white hands. Did you know that the sea turtle's flippers contain the same bones as our limbs, the long limb bones shrunken and shortened, the bones of the wrists and ankles widened and flattened?

Clambering back on to the boat, I realize I have received a gift.

Not everyone feels so.

"Well," says a fellow diver, pulling off his mask, "that was about as boring as it gets."

For a moment I wonder if he was on the same dive, so I helpfully mention the plethora of turtles.

Of course, he saw them.

"I saw a million," he says. "Which was a million too many."

I hoped he was finished, but he wasn't.

"And they swim like they're stoned. I mean, I've never seen anything move so *slow*."

It is commonplace in life, two divergent takes on the same thing -- anyone who has watched television news, or entered into matrimony knows this – but for an instant I am surprised. But in life we are presented with choices, and each of us make our own.

Albert Einstein once said, "There are only two ways to live your life. One is as though nothing is a miracle. The other is as though everything is a miracle."

I am an ardent admirer of observers, and so I am an admirer of poet and novelist Robert Penn Warren.

Warren was prolific. He wrote many things. Including this.

Black of grackles glints purple as, wheeling in sun-glare,
The flock splays away to pepper the blueness of distance.
Soon they are lost in the tracklessness of air.
I watch them go. I stand in my trance.

Goose-pimplingly lovely, isn't it? It's the opening of a poem called "Grackles Goodbye" by Mr. Warren, a man who always cast a keen eye on what he beheld. Grackles, you may know, are about as common-looking a bird as you'll find. They are also loud and aggressive, and eat pretty much anything: farmers and tillers of backyard gardens hate them because of their voracious appetite for seed and grain. But Warren saw the miracle of their annual migration and, beneath that surface, the mark of seasons passing.

Pay close attention, as Warren did, and you will see that "Grackles Goodbye" is also a poem about time and mortality, and the heartbreak and hard lesson that mortality ferries.

Grackles, goodbye! The sky will be vacant and
lonely
Till again I hear your horde's rusty creak high above,
Confirming the year's turn and the fact that
only, only,
In the name of Death do we learn the true
name of Love.

I believe Robert Penn Warren favored birds. "In my sleep," he wrote, "I continually dream of birds." In my own sleep, I often dream of sea turtles. I thought of Robert Penn Warren as I moved slowly through Sheraton Caverns, half dreaming. For, of birds, Warren also wrote…

Their eyes are round, boldly convex, bright as
a jewel,
And merciless. They do not know
Compassion, and if they did,
We should not be worthy of it. They fly
In air that glitters like fluent crystal
And is hard as perfectly transparent iron, they
cleave it
With no effort.

You see, don't you?

Much the same could be said about sea turtles.

Robert Penn Warren saw many things deeply and in this, he knew, he was graced. Paying close attention to this world, Warren once said, was "a way of existing meaningfully as much of your time as possible. And that's never much."

I should mention Robert Penn Warren was blind in one eye, courtesy of a long-ago rock thrown by a little brother.

Regarding seeing deeply, I myself am still a work in progress. I do not have to look deeply to see an example. The day before I lolled about Sheraton Caverns, I dove at a spot called Koloa Landing. Koloa Landing is also found off Poipu, quite close, actually, to Sheraton Caverns. A moderately strong swimmer could dispense with the boat ride and swim from one spot to the other.

To reach the wonders of Koloa Landing, you just walk out into the water. It's a few steps off the beach. Before we dove at Koloa Landing, we stood on the beach listening to our dive guide, a pretty, enthusiastic young lady named Sabine, give us a breathless run down of all the astonishing things we might see. Be sure, she effused, to look closely. We would have so many wonders to notch in our dive logs.

Frankly, the conditions didn't look too appealing. There had been a lot of rain, and beneath overcast skies, the waters of Koloa Landing were creamy brown. When Sabine and her enthusiasm were out of earshot, a fellow diver turned to me.

"We'll be lucky to see our damn hand," he said.

"If I do," I told him, "I'm putting it in my log book."

Well, metaphorical mud in both our faces. Beneath the murky waters we saw snowflake morays, a mustache conger eel, a blue dragon nudibranch, a devil scorpionfish, a flying gurnard and three yellow frogfish. You don't have to know what these creatures are (though I'd advise, for great fun, looking them up). You only have to know they are as stunning and bizarre as the wildest hallucinogenic dream. And, remembering to look beneath the surface, looks aren't everything. Frogfish resemble a malformed lump of clay, and, in open water, they swim like Irishmen at closing time. But do not dismiss the humble frogfish as laughable, for they are the fastest vertebrate predator on Earth. Wedged in a fissure of rock, dangling the lure that extends from just above its mouth, the frogfish draws its curious prey near, then inhales it in roughly one-sixth of a second.

Whenever I begin to dismiss something as commonplace, I think of my friend the frogfish. And then I pay very close attention.

It is true, sea turtles will not impress at Indy, but they are not a part of our hyperkinetic age. I am past the age where I feel the need to correct others -- for one thing they might be right -- but I believe, in questioning the green sea turtle's capacity for movement, my dive companion missed something.

There is a reason I dream of sea turtles.

Most people group sea turtles into one lump. There are actually eight species of sea turtles, from the massive leatherback to the diminutive Kemp's ridley. The leatherback can reach six and a half feet; the Kemp's ridley grows to thirty inches. But size doesn't matter, for each turtle is an otherworldly assemblage of instinct focused on survival. For the sea turtle, focus is a must. Leatherback, Kemp's ridley, green sea turtle, every hatchling that bursts from the sand has less than a one percent chance of reaching maturity. Even in the egg, they are set upon by fly larvae and fungi. Scrabbling across the sand, instants after coming into the world, they are attacked by birds, crabs, raccoons, rats, and a host of other opportunistic mammals, including man. And the sea waits, with its hungry minions. A thousand eggs are laid so that the one will survive.

Each hatchling bursts forth as if it is the chosen one. There is always the chance.

The miracle, and the exercise in belief, do not end at the water's edge. Plunging into the surf, the hatchling, no bigger than a child's hand, remains undaunted. Having never seen the ocean before, the turtle swims an unerring course, first through crashing surf, and then across the seas themselves, more blank and featureless than anything terra firma can conjure. How do they know what to do? Man isn't certain. Scientists have learned that on entering the surf, the hatchlings orient themselves in the direction of the incoming waves. Beyond the surf, in the great Gobi expanse, they are apparently guided by an inborn sense of magnetic direction. Of late, biologists believe that, in the case of the leatherback turtle, a patch of pale skin near the eye may allow light to reach the pineal gland, which in turn may inform the turtle of changes in the length of the days, cueing migration.

Whatever their means of navigation, the turtles swim, confident and alone. Turtles do not travel in pods or packs. Each is captain of its own fate. After wobbling into the waters off the beach of their birth, they swim for years, the few survivors feeding and growing, the rest struck down by sharks, disease, fishermen, drifting nets, and bits of plastic they mistake for jellyfish and ingest. It is a long list of pitfalls. Science does not know precisely where the turtles go. Tagging has revealed that a young leatherback might swim 7,000 miles, but we have never been able to fully track them as they mature to adulthood. *The lost years*, science calls them.

Biologists surmise that sea turtles require from ten to fifty years to mature and reproduce. When they are mature, on a signal we do not know, they veer in the darkness. For generations, villagers on beaches in Costa Rica, Venezuela, and Suriname claimed the same turtles returned to the beach of their birth. Science dismissed this primitive folklore. Now genetic evidence—the examination of distinctive mitochondrial DNA—suggests this is precisely what happens. How do they find their way back to the beach of their birth? Science doesn't know.

How can you not love when science is reprimanded by folklore? How can you not thrill to the sea turtle's magic and mystery? How can their dogged struggle not give you inspiration and faith?

I asked none of these questions of my disappointed dive companion.

We see different things.

I love all sea turtles, but if forced, I will admit that *Dermochelys coriacea* is my favorite. The leatherback turtle is remarkable. Seeking food, it can dive to nearly 4,000 feet. Three-quarters of a mile. Imagine the silence and salve in a world we will never know. Leatherback turtles have been spotted in frigid waters off Newfoundland, Norway, Chile, and New Zealand. In bone-chilling waters that would instantly kill their reptilian relations (and, very shortly thereafter, us), the leatherback shuts off the blood supply to its extremities, withdrawing inward, shepherding warmth and life. *Dermochelys coriacea* is not always easily kept in captivity. In aquariums, leatherbacks have banged up against the glass again and again, unable to comprehend the concept of a barrier. In one aquarium, the Plexiglas wall in question faced the sea. It is unabashed anthropomorphism, but I find something noble in this.

One last item, regarding sea turtles in general. They are one of the few animals that descended from land ancestors and returned to the sea.

I return to the sea in my dreams. The dreams vary, as dreams do, but there are often constants. In my dreams I swim easily in green waters, just below the surface so that the sky ripples overhead, the white clouds like bed sheets in the wind. I swim slowly, as a creature far beyond our time would do, but the passing water sings in my ears nonetheless, a lullaby that is serene and comforting. I sense something timeless, something beyond mankind's stumblings, passed to me in a whisper I cannot quite grasp, but it soothes me nonetheless. I am gripped by something that swings on the very hinges of the earth, something so large it erases any urge to conquer, to compete, to dominate, to prove, to possess, to hate, to question.

You can see why I like these dreams.

Robert Penn Warren spent much of his life in Tennessee, which is not rife with sea turtles. But I believe he would have enjoyed them very much. I believe he would have seen them for what they are.

Another of Einstein's miracles.

HUNTING GROUND

I saw my friend Steve Munch recently and this reminded me again of the surprise and raw beauty in this world, not to mention the lovely unfoldings and potential for visceral heartbreak that exist right off our noses.

Let me explain.

First let me say that Steve Munch is many things, many of which cannot see print, but above all he is a man who cares deeply about our oceans. He is also a supremely talented photographer. Steve photographs many things, but most of his photos center around the waters off the Southern California shoreline we both call home. Steve is not lackadaisical in his efforts. He spends over 200 days a year out on his boat shooting. This allows him some special moments.

I have been out on the water with Steve (not often enough for me, but perhaps too often for him), and I will tell you there is no finer way to spend a day. For one thing, Steve is a gifted storyteller. Like many gifted storytellers, Steve's reservoir of stories is deep. He has lived a varied life. He has sold roadside vegetables. He worked as a commercial fisherman. Plenty of stories there. One of my favorite fishing stories involves a vacuous crewman, a hatch left open, a rapidly sinking boat, a nighttime swim to shore and a cold night spent on a desolate island in skivvies. Steve appreciates humanity's absurdities, his own included. Nor does he shy away from telling it like it is. More than once, when Steve has called to invite me out on his boat, I myself have foundered, waffling, and making excuses like a job, forcing Steve to interrupt. "You're starting to piss me off, McAlpine. You're a little like a cow. I've got to prod you."

Steve knows I want to be out on the water. He does what he has to. Above all, Steve has a good heart.

Our home waters of the Santa Barbara Channel are rife with life, and it is not unusual to encounter this life the instant you leave shore. Not long ago Steve, having prodded me on to his boat, had us idling just outside the Ventura Harbor entrance, surrounded by a nursery pod of common dolphin. As the sun rose in the east, the water's surface, clenching the last of the pink, was like a mirror. The infant dolphins, roughly the size of an inflated football, burst from the slick water, executing the same perfect scimitar leaps as their elders, barely a splash on entry or exit. The only sounds punctuating the quiet were the chuffs of the dolphins, the sound like a snorkel being cleared. Steve was crouched and shooting. He owns two photo studios, and a good dolphin shot will put food on the table. But the moment was achingly beautiful, and Steve has never been about money. Nor does it matter that he has seen the same thing hundreds of times before.

"God," he whispered. "What a gift."

Leave any shore, and you can't help but be struck by the abrupt demarcation from the world we know, and the world we share. Beautiful, raw surprise, but, of course, not really a surprise at all.

And there are different moments of heartbreaking beauty. Steve's oceanic encounters are not all fairy tale moments of infant dolphins and ethereal light.

On this day, dolphins surprise Steve first, exploding from the Pacific like fistfuls of scattered birdseed, a pod maybe a thousand strong. Wildlife photography is a frustrating business, but there are rare times when the natural world aligns itself. On this bright morning hundreds of dolphins fleck the surface. Behind them, Southern California's Anacapa Island provides the perfect backdrop. It is a gift of timing and luck. Steve throws himself on the deck of the boat, getting as close to water level as possible, firing off shots of sleek forms rocketing from the water all around him. This is when he hears another noise, different from the oddly multi-directional leaping of the dolphins. This sound, the slightest hissing of parted water, is more unified, perhaps almost clinically efficient. Steve looks off the stern. The orcas, five or six of them, move nearly as one, each separated from the other by little over an arm's length. Steve breaks photography's first commandment. He lowers his lens. *Oh my god.*

All playfulness dissolves from the day. This is no game. The whales move with lethal power. Slipping beneath the surface they make a sound like a whisper.

The bull explodes from the water, a dolphin in its mouth. The panicked pod of dolphins runs, undulating for the relative safety of the island. Steve recovers his wits and his professionalism. He brings the camera up again, steering the boat with his feet. His hands shake. It takes all his skill to keep the lens level.

Beauty now in a dark fashion. Expertly, the orcas separate four or five dolphins from the pod and begin their work. The culled dolphins break left. They break right. Their shadows flick beneath the water at astonishing speed. The orcas are often invisible, but it is clear what they're doing. It's terribly simple. They are exhausting their prey. The female orcas chase, herd and confuse the dolphins. Then the bull comes up from beneath and finishes them.

At the end there are two dolphins left. They come to Steve's boat, the only cover in the open water, pressing against the hull. There is nowhere else for them to hide.

In the quiet, the dolphins pant. Biologists believe dolphins are one of the few mammals that recognize impending death. Their fear is clear. As the orcas rise to the surface, Steve feels the water boiling through the transom.

Another dolphin disappears.

Wounded and exhausted, the last survivor lays just off the boat's swim step. Steve could reach out and touch the dolphin. Its panting is nearly human, a desperate runner at the end of a great race. Steve is torn between helping – is it even possible to roll the panicked dolphin on board? -- and doing what photographers do. Already he feels the seep of betrayal.

Nature allows no time for debate. There is nothing dramatic in this ending. The bull surfaces and rolls over on the dolphin, gently taking him down into the sea.

The boat settles. Steve waits. The dolphins and the orcas are gone. There is only haunting silence.

If you ask, my friend Steve will talk about this encounter. If you don't ask, he won't.

As I said, he has a good heart.

THE CURIOUS MATTER OF THE YONAGUNI RUINS

When we disembark at tiny Yonaguni airport, we are the only Europeans in the terminal. A small boy stares at me as if the top of my head has erupted in flame. I hand him my surfboard key chain. He returns a perfect small bow.

If you prefer small places to large (I do), you will fall in love with tiny, 11-square mile Yonaguni Island from your first salt-laced breath. The island chain that is Japan is enormous, stretching some 1,500 miles from north to south, more than 5,000 islands in all. Yonaguni (just east of Taiwan) is nearly lost at the chain's southernmost end. The island is home to three small maze-like towns huddled beside the water. The remainder of the island is a green mosaic of sugar cane fields, dripping jungle and grassy swards grazed by the miniature Yonaguni horse, which is only slightly larger than the Atlas moth, Yonaguni's other signature creature. Given the 800-some residents know where they're going, most street signs direct the visitor to lookouts, and a fine thing that is, for there are some knee-jellying stunners, from jungle vistas to craggy cliffs plummeting into leaping blue-green seas. You would have to be dizzy (*Memai ga shimasu*) not to see that Yonaguni swims in *aji* (character).

Everywhere is the sea, which suits many of the residents just fine.

"The sea connects the world," a young woman told me during our visit, or at least I think that's what she said, for when it comes to bridging the language barrier, much is indeed lost in translation. "When I look at the ocean it touches my heart." Here she touched her heart. She appeared to consider something, glanced shyly in the direction of her knees, and then issued another brief spout of Japanese.

Our translator turned to me.

"She says it is also very small here. She would like to visit New York."

Some 300 miles southwest of the main island of Okinawa, yet still a member of the Okinawa prefecture (think state), Yonaguni Island is *Ha Te* (the very far end), an appropriate location for a mystery unresolved.

We meet Kihachiro Aratake on our first day on the island. I am traveling with a group of American divers, and it is Kihachiro Aratake's discovery we have come to see, flying to Yonaguni from Ishigaki Island to the north, bumping to the tarmac in a small plane peopled mostly with locals who spend much of the flight bowing and smiling in our direction. In Okinawa's bustling capital city of Naha an American ex-pat told me that if I passed out drunk on the streets of Naha with a thousand dollars spilling from my trousers, I'd wake in the morning to find the bills tucked firmly back in my pocket. During my time on Yonaguni I came to see that, should the same fate befall a Yonaguni visitor, they would wake with their funds intact and a pillow under their head. And perhaps a small parting gift to ease the ache of overnighting on pavement.

Shurei no kokoro. Embrace all visitors and treat them with the utmost courtesy.

It is something to remember.

Like his fellow islanders, Kihachiro Aratake would prove gracious and generous to beyond a fault, but when we meet him for the first time, he sports a commanding manner and a stern gaze. Aratake is built much like his island, square and powerful, and a life as a fisherman hasn't done much to soften him up. While we slurp Yaeyamasoba (Yonaguni style noodles) and eat Soki Soba (pork spare rib cooked in soy sauce), further contributing to our own softness, Aratake declines lunch to hold court, speaking rapidly and decisively about our upcoming visit to his famed Yonaguni ruins. Aratake favors stripes, and he is wearing the sort of black and white striped shirt once worn by Popeye. This makes him look broader still, and as he speaks, jabbing at the map before him like an angry mime, our translator scurries to keep up. Aratake's work-bludgeoned fingers trace unintelligible arcs across the map's surface, unintelligible because our translator has given up. Aratake keeps talking though, only now he appears to be mildly amused. He also appears to fix his dark eyes on me, probably because I have made the mistake of sitting directly across from him.

When we dive we will perform a human sacrifice, perhaps with the skinny one.

When he finishes talking, he rolls up the map.

Reaching across the table, he taps my forearm decisively.

"We go diving," he says in perfect English. "Then you decide."

Here's the thing. These ruins that Kihachiro Aratake discovered, no one knows if they are a geologic formation or something man-made. This debate would be an off-the-radar quibble, but for one thing. This structure that Kihachiro Aratake discovered, known locally as Yonaguni Monument, it is not inconsequential. Measuring some 500 feet long by 80 feet wide, it is eight stories tall.

There are many things in this world that hide from us, some just beneath the surface. Until 1985 the Yonaguni ruins (ruins can be geologic or man-made; and they sound a lot more exciting than Monument) were one of them. That was the year Aratake headed out to scout the southernmost tip of Yonaguni Island for the hammerhead schools he hoped might serve as an anchor for a dive business. What he found instead surprised the world, and the bickering hasn't stopped since.

Aratake runs his own dive outfit, Sa-wes Yonaguni. Fittingly, he takes us out to see the ruins himself.

The ruins are fifteen minutes from Yonaguni's harbor. It was sunny earlier – Okinawa prefecture's 160-some islands are closer in climate to Tahiti than they are to Tokyo -- but swiftly the day has taken on a blustery, black look. The seas are rough. On the ride out, Aratake's boat bangs against the swell, and several of our group assume pasty complexions. It seems to me that Aratake's eyes have again taken on their amused light, although all amusement disappears when we arrive at the dive site in the additional shadow of hundred-foot cliffs. It is even rougher here. Yonaguni benefits from the full brunt of the Kuroshio Current, which brings in swordfish and tuna for fishermen, and, for divers, giant cuttlefish, barracuda and the occasional school of 100-plus hammerheads, the latter massing in winter to breed.

It can also produce leaping seas.

Aratake does not anchor. He will stay with the boat, while one of his dive guides shepherds us below the water. The boat putters in the turmoil, Aratake, at the helm, trying to avoid being broadsided by the biggest of the waves. We divers are already rigged and ready. Having already taken our measure, Aratake had us gear up in the harbor. One by one, we leap into the sea. This process goes smoothly until a member of our group has her mask slapped loose by the roguish waves. Mildly panicked, she swims to the steel ladder dangling off the back of the boat.

We spent the previous week diving off the main island of Okinawa. There, if we committed some diving faux pas (and we did), post-dive we received a polite reprimand. *Please. Ken-san. We want more attention from you.* Aratake is not of this school. He is yelling now with all his chesty bluster, and we don't need a translator to see he is unhappy and with good reason, for the swim ladder bangs wildly against the stern, and the woman in question, having now grabbed one of the rungs, is in sore danger of having a wholesale dental realignment.

I will not say Aratake kicks her off the ladder, but I will say he strongly encourages her to let go. When she does, our dive guide grabs the woman by the arms and sidestrokes her away from the boat. Before we descend, the last thing I see is Aratake hopping up and down, Popeye ranting. But water silences man's noise, and as we drop beneath the surface, even the boisterous Aratake disappears.

As I said, these ruins that Aratake discovered are not inconsequential. Given they rise almost eight stories, the tops of the ruins are only about twenty feet below the surface. In these shallows we are removed from surface waves, but the surge still sweeps us back and forth over the strange stone shapes like neoprene metal detectors. The overcast day thrusts its shadows deep into the water.

Overhead the breaking waves make dark, roiling storm clouds on the surface.

It is the perfect atmosphere for something mysterious, and as we go deeper the sense of mystery, well, deepens. I have forgotten the turmoil above. I have forgotten my fellow divers. Finning through shadow, I see evidence of the debate with my own eyes. Everywhere I turn, stone is cleft at sharp, perfect angles. Here something like an arch. There something very much like steps. There are waist-high passageways (dwarves?), and, on some of the expansive flat surfaces, conical borings in the rock (dwarves with time on their hands?). Looking down into these borings is like staring down a throat.

Some formations are crude enough that they might not be carved. Others look like the chiseling just wrapped up before we descended. Steps along the side of the monolith make perfect right angles. At sixty feet I swim through a jumble of stones that might or might not be an archway, and then I come upon two perfectly formed stone rectangles. Each rectangle is over twenty feet tall. They are perfectly aligned. Side by side, they nearly touch. In the deep blue, shadows snake about them. Something performs a similar goose-pimpling along my spine. Later, in the course of additional research, I will learn that Professor Masaaki Kimura, perhaps the foremost expert on the Yonaguni Monument, believes the four-inch gap between the two massive stone rectangles may have channeled a shaft of sunlight signaling the autumn equinox. I will also learn that many disagree with Professor Kimura on this and many other points.

Geologic or man-made, here beneath the water there is something decidedly altar-like about the entire structure. I cannot cast a vote either way, doubt and certainty buffet me in waves, but staring at the vast, smoky blue structure I am struck by one surety. It is easy to sense something bigger than man.

I am required to stay with the group, but having already ignored that decree, it is easier still to fin away to a place where I am wholly alone. Finding a still, current-free spot at the foot of a sheer wall, I go to my knees and, with my current country of residence in mind, bow in gratitude for the chance to witness something far beyond the daily pale.

My meditation is interrupted by a clanging. I look up slowly because I know what I am going to see. Our dive guide has stopped banging his knife against his tank. Now he is waving it at me, gesturing for me to join the others. I have had my moment. I am willing to face the wrath of Aratake. Placing my hand flat against the wall, I say a silent farewell and ascend.

What is certain about the Yonaguni ruins is they were discovered by Kihachiro Aratake, and Aratake did not miss the moment of the moment.

"When I first saw it I had goose bumps and feel strange wondering why something like this exists underwater," Aratake told a crew from the History Channel's "History's Mysteries."

I know this because Aratake shows us the video that night in his guesthouse, Hotel Irifune Bamboo Villa. He has already served us a lavish meal of shrimp, sashimi and other seafood delicacies that look more like art than food. There has also been plenty of the local awamori, a drink of liquid that is closer to flame, downed with shouts of "Hai!" Many of us now are. The local literature describes Yonaguni's awamori as strong enough to help prevent heart attacks. To me this seems no laudable feat when your heart has already stopped.

I drink the awamori sparingly. Through sometimes hard experience, I have found that it is easier to learn from an upright position. I notice that on this night Aratake is a teetotaler too. Ever the gracious host, he quietly watches this video he has no doubt seen dozens of times. Aratake has invited friends. They, too, raptly watch the video as if they have never seen it before.

In the video various experts snipe at each other.

"It appears to be a huge ritual religious area that predates the Egyptian pyramids by 5,000 years, making it the oldest structure in the world, forcing a possible revision of history," says one.

"Just because it looks like history, doesn't mean it is," carps another.

Staring intently into the camera another expert says, "There was just a sense about the place. You felt that other people had been there before," which strikes me as a bit unscientific but rather accurate.

We continue watching, though two of my companions are already sleeping on Aratake's couches. There is much that is complicated – geologic terms, carbon-dating, an undercurrent of snitty scientific name calling – but the argument boils down to a simple one. Is the structure man-made, or is it the result of geology?

None of the experts interviewed in the video can reach agreement, so when the video is over I turn and ask Aratake himself.

As the translator directs my question to Aratake the room falls silent.

Aratake absorbs the question. He regards me for a long moment, stoic and heavy-lidded. It seems to me that the translator uses an excessive amount of verbiage to relay a simple question. Earlier in the evening, when I had asked one of his English-speaking friends if Aratake was still a fisherman, the friend had replied, "He is a pirate." Aratake had not hesitated to kick the panicked woman from the ladder. For all I knew the translator had just said, *This is the one who thinks he is beyond the rules.* Aratake's guest house sits high on a hill, at the top of a very long fall.

And so the world is still, and then Kihachiro Aratake smiles a 12-year-old boy's smile, and light spills into his dark eyes, light tinged, possibly, with a trace of awe. Spreading his rough hands on the low table between us, Aratake speaks slowly and definitively, his words producing murmurs and nods of agreement among the Japanese speakers at the table.

The translator turns to me.

"Yes, it is fantastic. Everything is so calculated and even, all the angles so perfect. Everything is so beautiful whether it's natural or manmade."

That night, after we return to the hotel and my companions exchange couch for bed, I leave the hotel and walk beneath the stars. Being Yonaguni, forty steps puts me beyond civilization's touch. I walk along the empty road. There are no streetlights. It is just the sound of the sea, attended to by the heavens.

I mull over the debate a last time, and then I release it to the stars.

I never really wondered if the Yonaguni ruins are man-made or natural.

What puzzles me is why man has to label everything.

ONE SALTY TALE

On the Eastern Shore of Virginia I met Jerry Doughty, who told me the beginnings of the story of George Avery Melvin with characteristic aplomb.

"An interesting case, the Melvin family," Jerry said in a monotone outdone only by his bland expression. "It was a spectacular news story around here."

In our time together, I came to like Jerry Doughty for many reasons, not the least of which was his ability to recount even the most fascinating story in the same animated tone flight attendants use to explain how your seat belt works. In this day and age of Tell All, Jerry also told me what I needed to know, and what I didn't need to know. In our time together exploring small towns the likes of Willis Wharf, Machipongo and Exmore, Jerry recounted tales of suicides, curses, incestuous relations and other assorted scandals, almost always pulling up short of the end to regard me stone-faced.

"You can't believe it. I wish I could tell you more, but I can't."

Jerry favored brown polyester slacks, a thin brown jacket, a ball cap to tame his wild gray hair, and a pair of worn New Balance sneakers. He was born in the Eastern Shore town of Nassawadox in

1944, taught U.S. History at middle school for over thirty years, and never left this place he loved. A sepia photograph places his great-great-great grandfather Martin Doughty on nearby Hog Island around 1882. At one time Jerry's family owned Hog Island. This Jerry Doughty volunteered eventually.

And Hog Island is where the curious tale of George Avery Melvin unfolded.

These days Hog Island is a lovely place, bereft of man, home to empty beaches, brushy tangles of wild blackberry and wax myrtle, and flocks of birds that wheel in the sky as one, their collective undersides producing a sudden, shimmering white veil not unlike a brief magical portal – except you don't want to leave the place where you're standing.

But this emptiness was not always so. In the early 1900s, Hog Island was home to the bustling town of Broadwater, a thriving community of some 250 people, with sixty-plus homes, a church, three general stores, a post office and an ice cream parlor. Today, with the exception of a few pilings, most of Broadwater rests beneath the Atlantic Ocean. Hog Island simply slowly walked out from beneath Broadwater. Today's Hog Island is roughly the same size it always was – about six miles long and a mile and a half wide – only now it is farther west. When the sand moved, the town of Broadwater couldn't.

George Avery Melvin was repositioned a bit more suddenly. Jerry told me most of George Avery Melvin's story, and what he didn't tell me, Rick Kellam finished.

Jerry began, rightly, with geology. Islands, he pointed out, are impractical places to bury the deceased. The soil isn't deep, and what soil there is often has a water table pushing right up against it.

"When a storm of consequence passes through," Jerry told me, "the caskets are washed free."

And so it was with the Great Storm of 1933. Churning floodwaters rushed over the island, sweeping away great trees and raising more than caskets up into the light.

"We looked down in the rushing water," recalled an island resident of the time, "and everywhere we looked there were snake heads sticking up out of the water."

Among the rearing snake heads bobbed the coffins, including the coffin of George Avery Melvin. Jerry told me that on Hog Island, post-storm, the first order of business was to look for the living. The second was to retrieve the already deceased. However, after the Great Storm of 1933, George Avery Melvin would not be found. At least not quickly.

I heard the rest of the story from Rick Kellam, who took me out to Hog Island on his twenty-four-foot Carolina skiff. This was only fitting because Rick Kellam is the sort of gracious person who will take a stranger for a boat ride. He is also George Avery Melvin's great grandson. By Rick's own estimates, his first ancestor set foot on Hog Island in the mid-1700s.

The day Rick and I set foot on Hog Island, it was sunny and blue when we left Willis Wharf, and prettier still when Rick maneuvered his skiff into a shallow gut at the south end of the island.

Little known fact. Twenty-three barrier islands lie just off Virginia's Eastern Shore. The most famous of these is Chincoteague (home to the famed ponies of the same name), but there are plenty of islands you've never heard of – sing-song names like Metompkin, Mockhorn, Parramore, and Assawoman – and they are so rare and beautiful that the United Nations has declared the islands an International Biosphere Reserve.

Hog Island is part of this otherworldly sandy pearl string, and few know Hog Island as well, or appreciate it as much, as Rick Kellam.

Settling the anchor in the muck, Rick surveyed the blue sky, the sleepy tidal waters, and the sea of marsh grass rippling with its own currents in the slight breeze.

"There really is heaven on earth," he declared.

Two rows of pilings, neatly paralleling each other, ran low across the marsh.

Rick followed my gaze.

"This was the Hog Island Hotel," Rick said, gesturing at the unimpressed marsh. "Those pilings were part of the walkway that led to the hotel. That's all that's left."

Donning waders, we squelched through the marsh muck. Attaining slightly higher ground, we followed a dusty path winding into the island's interior.

"Walking up this road, you'd be walking toward Broadwater," Rick said.

Except for a few lonely clumps of small, wind-stomped black pines, there were almost no trees.

When I made the obvious observation, Rick grinned.

"Right where we're walking was once smothered in a great maritime forest," he said. "The trees were forty to fifty feet tall, huge tunnels of them that blotted out the sky. They were called lover's lanes. People could walk under the canopy and not see the sky."

I knew where the forest had gone, but it was still hard to fathom.

"Yep," said Rick. "The ocean washed it out to sea."

As we walked beneath a wide blue sky, inhaling a salty breeze unencumbered by trees, Rick pointed out other things the ocean had washed away. *Here were homes. Here was a store.* Real people lived here, and as the afternoon passed Rick told me about some of their lives too. Fishermen who worked the surrounding waters, young boys who stuffed pumpkins down toilets, young girls and boys who sat close around bonfires, barely watching the oysters roasting on the end of their wires. It was a hard life on many fronts, with little of society's luxuries. Rick told me that when the Hog Islanders went to the mainland, they'd often fill their pockets with the wafer thin shells scattered in plentitude along their beaches. Strolling about on the mainland, they'd shake their hands in their pockets and the shells would make a jingle like coins. "So that no one would think they were poor," Rick said.

Rick also told me the last piece of George Avery Melvin's story.

George Avery Melvin was buried on Hog Island because that's where he lived, though frankly he was so frugal he would likely have preferred to be left where he dropped.

"He was so tight, he probably wouldn't have even wanted a box," Rick said cheerily. "He was an irascible fellow who didn't like spending money."

But it is life's final twist that when you are dead you can't argue your cause, and so his family buried him in a pine box, though, also inclined to his ways, they buried him in a pine box that came easily open. When the Great Storm of 1933 nearly washed Hog Island away, George Avery Melvin surfaced like a whack-a-mole, bobbed about wildly, and then floated off for points unseen for twenty-some years.

Rick, like Jerry, wasn't big on histrionics, though Rick did grin slightly when he found things amusing.

"It was in the 1950s, on Rogue's Island, a half mile south of Hog Island. A Coast Guardsman and a local waterman were walking the backside of the island scavenging after a storm. They were walking along the inland marsh side of the island and looked down. One looked at the other and said, 'I believe that's George Avery Melvin.' He wasn't hard to recognize. He still had on his coat and tie and white shirt. The only thing that had changed was that his hair and fingernails had grown. From the day he was buried until the day he was found, he was probably immersed in salt water. His body had literally turned to stone. He was petrified by the salt content in the water. The Smithsonian sent representatives who wanted to take his body to Washington to examine it, but my grandmother refused."

That left the matter of re-disposal. Frugality still coursing through the family veins, family balked at the price of a casket. The director of the funeral parlor presented a workable option. George was already missing part of one leg up to the knee, and he was stiff as stone.

"They chiseled off the other leg and put him in a baby coffin," said Rick. "He was a short fellah anyway."

Rick and I walked for a time in silence. Perhaps we were considering our own mortality. Arriving atop a dune, we gazed down at a vast arc of beach, the velvet sand unmarked by footprints. Day was dimming, and the Atlantic Ocean followed suit, turning a deep blue in the falling light. Upon this deep blue surface deep blue waves rose and unfurled, their tops blown back in vapor-trail wisps by the light offshore breeze.

I could hear Rick breathing beside me.

The storm that saw to George Avery Melvin's departure wasn't why Hog Island was so silent now.

Rick spoke quietly to the darkening Atlantic.

"It really wasn't the 1933 storm that put an end to Broadwater," he said. "The main reason people left Hog Island was modern conveniences: electricity, heat, running water, movie theaters. They were beat down and tired of not having what everybody else had."

Rick regarded the sliver of moon.

"Technology was what destroyed Broadwater."

BREATHLESS

It is an unnerving thing to find yourself unable to breathe in a dark, confined space: slightly more unnerving still when those dark confines are 90 feet beneath the ocean's surface in a world of silty silence and sad endings. Amidst the natural glories of the island nation of Palau, life has, will, and can take sudden and unexpected turns. Life is like that.

It is also true that small things can add up to big things, sometimes very quickly. You might be on a dive boat drifting upon some of the most beautiful seas in the world. Lovely seas, peaceful seas, seas of sunshine and sapphire blue that lull you into a sense of serenity that is very real, but may soon prove very false. You might explain to the guide on board the dive boat that your dive computer, that handy item that measures such consequentials as one's depth and remaining air, isn't working, and that you (because, in the end, alone and breathless in a dark place, it is very much your fault) neglected to bring a backup. You might expect special treatment of some degree because you are a fairly experienced diver and comfortable in the water. The guide, because guides are good at sensing such hubris, might offer that dispensation. On this second dive, you are told, you can descend without a dive computer. Just stay close to the guide and, using his functioning computer, he'll monitor his own air, assume your consumption is roughly the same, and surface plenty early to account for the fact that he probably uses less air than you. You might find this arrangement quite agreeable, because everyone is about to dive a World War II wreck, and you love to dive on wrecks.

You might absently reach for a tank.

And in that innocuous, and careless, reaching, everything bad – and good – falls into place.

The island nation of Palau is located east of the Philippines and north of New Guinea: 340 some islands scattered across roughly 400 miles of Western Pacific. The Helmet Wreck is located at the bottom of Malakal Harbor, a very short boat ride from Palau's capital city of Koror. The ship, roughly 190 feet long, rests upright on the sloping bottom, with her bow (110 feet beneath the surface) lower than her stern (45 feet below the surface). The original name of the vessel has been lost in the mists of time. Some believe she was confiscated by the Japanese, and then sent to the bottom by the Americans courtesy of the gaping hole on her aft starboard side, a tremendous explosion that tore open the hull so that today the ribs of the ship are clearly exposed and depth charges are scattered about in the sand. That's right, the depth charges are still there. As are stacks of helmets (cemented together now by corals and corrosion), piles of rifles and ammunition, a scattering of ceramic sake bottles and, here and there, a gas mask staring unblinking up into the blue.

That's the thing about the ocean. It doesn't forget the past.

Unless you are an imbecile, the Helmet Wreck is not a dangerous place. Just in case you are an imbecile, the dive operators who visit the wreck are clear. "DO NOT PICK UP ANY AMMUNITION!!!!! These pieces of history are very unstable and can explode," read the brochures – and the truth is, the silent ammunition emanates a very palpable menace. These were instruments of killing, denied their function because their overseers were killed first. But here they are, waiting.

Mostly, the Helmet Wreck is a sobering place. Men died here: terribly and suddenly, or terribly and slowly. We will never know. The dive operators who come to this wreck with their buzzing customers issue another warning regarding the Helmet Wreck, and they are wise to do so.

The attractions on this wreck may cause distractions.

Indeed.

We descend down the mooring line, and arrive at the bow of the Helmet Wreck. Her decks and hull are covered with thick layers of coral, the patience of invisible polyps grown highly visible over the years. I see shoes and boots half buried in silt. It is eerie and sad – for you and I wear shoes and boots too.

It is a mistake, but I want to be alone. We have only been down for five minutes. I have plenty of air left. I signal the guide. There is an inner passageway through the wreck, and that is where I want to go. Most of the other divers are outside the wreck, finning about the deck. The guide is responsible for them too. He gives me the okay sign. I return it. We are thinking the same thing. Ten minutes inside the ship, and then I will come out and find him. I have at least forty minutes of air. I drop through a hole in the deck, and enter a world that has thumbed its nose at time.

Here is the thing about wrecks. They are hypnotizing. Inside a wreck the silent embrace of water – always soothing – is magnified. The silence is deeper. The water itself seems thicker and more viscous, often nearly milky. Psychology is also at play. Wrecks pulse with emotion, highlighting our fragility and impermanence in the face of forces greater than us. And the truth is, for the unabashedly childish, wrecks are really cool fun. You fly about the interior like Peter Pan, soaring through cabins and hovering over catwalks, and if you are truly juvenile (I am), when you find your way into the wheelhouse, you stop and stand at the helm and bark orders to no one, peering commandingly out through the once windows at a blue horizon hung not with birds but with passing clouds of fish.

I am not alone in my fascination with wrecks. Divers from around the world flock to Palau and, just to the north, Chuuk, where there are dozens of wrecks -- an estimated 200,000 tons of equipment – destroyed, in part, by U.S. bombers in February 1944 over just two days.

War, in some cases, is necessary, but necessary or no, it never leaves us. Once I descended to the wreck of an American destroyer, sent to the bottom by the kamikaze plane who crashed through her hull. My fellow Western divers swam in and out of this gaping wound. Some of them probably just viewed it as a curiosity. Some of them might have said a silent prayer. I did. I also noticed that a young Japanese girl in our group avoided the gaping hole entirely. In fact, she stayed well off the wreck. We had been diving together for a week, and we had become friends. Back on board, when I alluded to her reluctance she spoke quietly. "My grandfather's brother was a kamikaze pilot," she said. "When I go on the wreck it is different for me."

Inside the Helmet Wreck I follow a viscous corridor. There is little light. The gray dimness blurs present and past. I pause and peer down into the engine room. I see more shoes and boots. That they have rested here for over seventy years is very strange. It is sad to think their owners never again laced them up and enjoyed a wink of those passing years. War takes the very young, and so the very young never know so many things.

And then I draw in on my regulator and it is difficult to breathe. On the next draw I get nothing.

In the silence I experience a wash of emotions. The primary one is disbelief.

I will not make this overly dramatic. I was never in real danger. It was just a matter of taking a figurative deep breath, calmly finding an exit and calmly swimming to the first diver I could find. If you're a diver you know this, but if you're not a diver you may not. Every diver carries a second breathing apparatus. Should a needy diver (like me) approach, the savior simply extends this breathing apparatus and both divers breathe from the same tank.

In the dusky-dark cavern of the Helmet Wreck, I told myself a simple and true thing. Thirty seconds maybe. A minute at most. Easily done, but for the squeeze of rising panic.

I found my way to an opening -- how long it took, I don't know: an eternity? – and when I exited out into the blue, I tried not to swing my head madly about. Even at the edge of panic, man does not want to appear a doofus. And there was my dive guide regarding me curiously, for perhaps my head was swinging wildly about. I made the sign for out of air -- think slashing your throat -- but it was probably unnecessary because I was finning toward him as if they had suddenly made reconnecting with your dive buddy an Olympic sport. He calmly handed me his second air hose and then, bound together like intimate dancers, we rose slowly to the surface.

Back on board, standing in sunshine that felt just a little bit warmer than it had before, we both deduced the problem. I had selected a nearly empty tank. Without a dive computer I had no way of knowing this, until I couldn't breathe.

I love the ocean. I was nearly born in it (see Father), and I didn't even come close to dying in it. But that night I still walked down to the ocean's edge, waded into the balmy tropical water, and swam out in the direction of the horizon. I didn't swim far, maybe a few hundred yards, and then I rolled over on my back and stared up at the stars. I didn't think of my wife or my sons back in California. I didn't think of myself, although the thudding of my heart in my chest felt immeasurably good. Staring up at the stars, I thought of the Japanese servicemen whose boots and shoes I had seen, and I wondered what it felt like to know, as your lungs fill with water, that there is no help at all.

During my stay in Palau I later heard a story. I would like to tell it to you now. It involves a gentleman named Tomimatsu Ishikawa. Mr. Ishikawa was a young man in 1944 when, as the Chief Engineer of the fleet-oiler Iro, his boat was attacked by American bombers off Palau. It was a sudden, unexpected turn, the American's surprise attack. It was called Operation Desecrate One. One moment sunshine and the cries of jungle birds. The next, the drone of planes. In the instant the bomb hit the engine room, Tomimatsu Ishikawa lost the fifteen men he commanded. He himself stumbled through smoke-clogged passageways, fighting to keep his footing in oil and blood. Reaching the deck he jumped into the lagoon. He was picked up by a patrol craft several hours later. The Iro burned for several days before it went to the bottom.

When Tomimatsu Ishikawa returned to Palau again he was in his mid-eighties. He was old, and an awkward diver, but, accompanied by curious divers, Palau's then Minister of Justice, and his own personal Japanese dive guide, Tomimatsu Ishikawa dove down to the Iro and performed a sacred sake ceremony on the aft deck of his ship. When the ceremony was complete, Tomimatsu Ishikawa rose up slowly beside the coral encrusted mast. At one point he stopped, and puzzled divers watched as his dive guide eventually pulled him away.

Why he stopped is anybody's guess, but the person who told me the story had one. Upon the mast, at about the point where Tomimatsu Ishikawa paused, an anemone had fixed itself to the mast.

The storyteller gave a slight smile.

"I've seen the anemone," he said. "It's beautiful. One of the most beautiful anemones I've ever seen. Maybe he saw it as something special. In a place of death, new life."

I nodded when the storyteller told me this. I agreed because I loved the poetry of the story, and the thought of a man who would be able to exchange death for life. I also agreed with him because the day before I had dove down to the Iro, following in Tomimatsu

Ishikawa's fin steps by just a few months. Rising to the surface, finning up alongside the mast, I had stopped dead in the water.

The anemone, its tentacles moving in the current like flowing silk, was the purest white.

The memory still leaves me breathless.

WHITE SHARK

On this October morning a wan sun baths silky blue waters. Two other boats are anchored off Isla Guadalupe, gleaming white playthings dwarfed by Guadalupe's volcanic hulk. Gray clouds crawl down the high ridgelines, the only movement on an island stony and bleak. To the horizon, all else is the sea. The feel is Jurassic Park, appropriate given what awaits us.

It took us 18 hours to get here, the 112-foot Solmar V departing from Ensenada, Mexico at one-thirty the preceding afternoon and motoring 165 miles through the night, anticipation building like thunderheads, the Russians boisterously toasting our upcoming adventure before everyone retired to their berths for the night.

Now that our moment has arrived, everyone is quiet.

It is possible a few of the Russians are hung over.

Standing on the deck in his wetsuit Arne Brockhaus fairly quivers. Arne is German. Ours is a multi-national group, drawn to a single flame.

"Since I am ten years old I want to see the white sharks," Arne says. "I have waited thirty years. This morning I wake up with my heart pounding."

My heart gallops too. No one, not even Lawrence Groth, who heads Great White Adventures and has journeyed to Guadalupe 180 times, is immune.

A massive form rolls to the surface, casually taking the football-size tuna head affixed to one of two ropes trailing off the stern. A desultory tug and the rope parts. The tuna head was supposed to be yanked away by the crew man holding the rope, but the crew man never saw this shark, an impressive sleight of hand for an animal 14 feet long.

As the white shark slips beneath the water, Lawrence Groth nods appreciatively.

"They're smart," he says. "They know we pull the line in to the boat when we see them coming, so they come in from under the boat to take the bait. They're problem solvers. Six hundred million years. They survived the last five extinction periods."

Fascinating, but we are not in the mood for a prolonged lecture. We wait, buzzing greyhounds behind a gate.

The water is still, telling no secrets.

Groth doesn't miss the smell of neoprene and sweat, or the antic adjusting and readjusting of mask straps. He appreciates a twist.

"Yep," he grins. "One of the few places in the world where somebody yells 'Shark!' and everybody jumps into the water."

Groth is a big man with broken-nail hands who looks like the commercial diver he once was. He can be gruff and abrupt, particularly when it comes to matters of safety. He has never had an accident in his years of commercial shark diving, and he doesn't plan to start this morning. The Russians, who sport T-shirts that proclaim *Another Beer Please, My Friend is Still Ugly* and require no excuse to hoist a drink, present a small dilemma. Groth has already had to lecture them this morning. Groth has only two rules -- don't drink and dive, and don't pet the animals – and the Russians have already broken one of them. One of their troupe, who saluted dawn with a beer, will not be diving today. The rest of the Russians stand chagrined but anxious.

Alex Lunev is their ring leader. Over the course of the next three days, Alex will also become my friend. Alex has already told me that he lives in the same Moscow neighborhood as Russian President Vladimir Putin, and he is not at all happy with how Putin's motorcade produces neighborhood gridlock. Alex is smart, funny and capable of incisive analysis. As we approached Guadalupe at dawn, he turned to me and decreed, "Eeees good island for monk."

Alex likes his vodka and his good times, but he now stands straight and stalwart as an Eagle Scout.

When Groth turns away, Alex leans close to me.

"In," he whispers. "I want go *in*."

Groth gives the Russian collective a last stern look.

"Okay," Groth says. "The first group can go."

One by one, we crawl crab-like on to the roof of the two cages affixed at water-level to the stern. One by one, we drop through the open hatches.

The silence of water closes over our heads.

I go to my knees on the bottom of the cage. Largely, this is functional: it keeps me from elbowing (and being elbowed by) my excitable fellow divers. But honestly, it is also a display of gratitude. I, too, have waited a lifetime for this. I peer, dry-mouthed and jittery, into the hazy blue. It isn't fear I feel, although there is certainly a touch of apprehension. It is honeymoon anticipation, the realization that I am about to receive a rare gift, the chance to glimpse a world older than anything I know, to see one of the world's greatest predators in its realm. Kong summoned.

I grasp the bars, a small boy peering through a window at something he never dreamed he would see.

The shark is less impressed. It rises slowly from beneath the cage, assuming form as it draws closer, although we all know the silhouette before it appears, for no other animal so occupies our imagination. Twelve feet long and wine cask thick, the shark turns and passes three feet from the front of the cages, elegant and largely indifferent, although its eye -- not black and soulless, but curious -- tracks us, eight burbling, bumbling neoprene forms falling about in the cages like inebriated astronauts.

Then -- and this is the part that will never cease to surprise me during our three days of gawping at Isla Guadalupe -- the shark angles down into the blue and disappears, dissolving as easily as a dream.

Shadow into shadow.

A living poem.

White shark cage diving takes place off the Farallon Islands off San Francisco, in South Africa, and in South Australia, but in these places it can be a frustrating affair. The water is often cold and murky. Many times the sharks don't appear. White sharks are one of the least predictable creatures on the planet, answering only to their own mysterious needs. How long do they live? Where do they breed? Where do they go in their open ocean travels? Man doesn't know.

But every year – every year since man has been paying attention -- from roughly June through November, white sharks congregate in the clear blue waters off Isla Guadalupe, their appearance (to date) as reliable as the rising sun. The reason is easy to hear, see, and, if the wind is blowing offshore, smell. During the summer and fall months northern elephant seals – and their naïve pups – inhabit the island, filling the air with their plaintive cries and guttural croakings, and filling the sharks' bellies with a blubber-rich buffet. In eleven years, and the aforementioned 180 trips, not once has Groth been skunked. Until the sharks decide otherwise, Guadalupe presents the rare white shark given.

"They're always here," Groth told me, the two of us seated at a table in the warmly lit main cabin as the Solmar V plied through a world of dark water and bright stars. "Guadalupe Island is the best place in the world for white shark diving. Period."

It was Groth who first dipped cages into Guadalupe's waters back in 2001. Groth had heard stories from San Diego's recreational fishing boats, journeying to Guadalupe to fish for the tuna that congregate there. Here was a place where white sharks swam in clear blue waters, and boisterously wrenched tuna from the fishermen's lines. When Groth pulled up with his first cages in 2001, he knew immediately that white shark diving had forever changed.

"We weren't even settled on the anchor yet and we had our first white shark. Three minutes. I knew that I had made the biggest discovery in shark diving history."

These days only a small number of shark diving outfitters are allowed out to Guadalupe. Permitted by the Mexican government, their presence is a winning proposition for white sharks and man. The Mexican government has declared Isla Guadalupe a protected area, but it is difficult to police an island more than a dozen horizons from shore. Instead the cage diving outfitters do it, keeping poachers, who could easily decimate the island's white shark population (the jaws, teeth and fins fetch a high price), at bay. The cage diving operators also provide funding and supplies (including cold beer) to the white shark researchers on Guadalupe (the waterless island is uninhabited but for a small Mexican naval base and a white shark research station: the latter no more than a weather-thrashed hut.).

Some of the outfitters also keep detailed records of their encounters with the sharks, and none are more detail-oriented than Groth and his crew. Often the same sharks return to Guadalupe year after year. Groth and his crew have identified them, catalogued them, named them (Cal Ripfin has his own facebook page), filmed them, and fallen under their spell.

Placing his thick forearms on the table, Groth leans forward and fixes his gaze on me.

"These are my friends. This is my family. It's very important to respect these animals."

Groth cares deeply for the sharks, and he has been doing what he can to help understand and protect them. His videographers have compiled hundreds of hours of white shark footage, footage viewed by researchers around the world in hopes of gleaning clues to the mysterious beasts. And the sharks need protection. It's an oft-bantered fact, but it bears re-bantering. Less than 500 people have died from shark attacks over the past 500 years, but humans kill an estimated 100 million sharks a year. White sharks are not removed from this spree.

It is a profoundly sad affair which, for better or worse, I once witnessed first-hand. Aboard a boat off the Galapagos, we came upon a fishing vessel. The three men aboard the vessel were working industriously, stacking the shark fins they had just hacked away. When our boat came close, I looked down into the shallow water. Sharks thrashed, finless, on the rocky bottom. It is an indelible memory, notched forever. Later I was told the fins were likely sold for shark fin soup.

Shark fins add virtually no flavor to the soup that bears their name. Their main purpose is to add gelatinous texture.

For a long time only researchers, a scattering of cage divers, and frustrated fishermen knew of Isla Guadalupe. But time has passed and social media has blossomed, and now, along with Cal Ripfin's facebook page, Youtube has brought Isla Guadalupe into humanity's light. There are many white shark videos. Not so long ago several videos of a female white shark known as Deep Blue went viral, under titles such as "Largest Shark Ever Recorded" and "GREATEST Great White Shark." One of the videos, taken by Guadalupe's own on-site scientist Mauricio Hoyos (who is as quietly understated as his video is grand), shows a shark of science fiction dimension, dwarfing a cage that looks like a child's toy. It is possible Deep Blue was pregnant, adding to her otherworldly girth. It is certain that she is between 19 and 21 feet long, one of the largest white sharks ever captured on film. Deep Blue is sighted at Guadalupe only rarely (which doesn't mean she isn't there more frequently). In the same month Mauricio Hoyos shot his footage, Discovery Channel videographers captured footage of Deep Blue too, using it later in a production titled "Jaws Strikes Back."

So it goes for white sharks, where bigger is better and a majestic creature who cares nothing for us is forever linked with a Peter Benchley book and Steven Spielberg movie.

Perhaps this is why, before descending into the cages, my friend Alex often salutes me and smiles.

"Das vedanya," he says.

Goodbye.

One of my favorite books is a dog-eared copy of *The Outermost House* by Henry Beston. In it Beston writes, "We need another wiser and perhaps more mystical concept of animals… We patronize them for their incompleteness, for their tragic fate of having taken form so far below ourselves. And therein we err, and greatly err. For the animals shall not be measured by man. In a world older and more complete than ours they move finished and complete, gifted with extensions of the senses we have lost or never attained, living by voices we shall never hear. They are not brethren, they are not underlings; they are other nations, caught with ourselves in the net of life and time, fellow prisoners of the splendor and travail of the earth."

This passage comes to mind every time I see a shark, and I have been graced to see more than my share. Some encounters have been brief. In Indonesia I jumped from a boat, nearly landing square on the back of a blacktip reef shark. Off the east coast of Australia a very large shark of indeterminate specie chased me from a desolate surf break (more accurately, I took it upon myself to madly windmill paddle to shore). Some of my encounters have been cloaked. Once, having just finished free diving off a murky pinnacle in the Sea of Cortez with friends far more experienced than me, I proclaimed my relief at having seen no sharks. One friend looked up idly from his beer. "Huh? They were everywhere." Other shark encounters have been gloriously vivid. Scuba diving in the Bahamas, I knelt on a white sand bottom and stared up into blue water not unlike sky as Caribbean reef sharks made ethereal loops. On the surface the wind blew, the breaking waves making a cloud cover beneath which the sharks flew. Ernest Hemingway fished in the Bahamas, and he saw his share of sharks. In *The Old Man and the Sea*, Hemingway wrote, "He is beautiful and noble and knows no fear of anything." To which I would only add, He – or she - has little to no interest in us.

We've all heard the statistics. If you take a dip in the ocean, there is a 1 in 11.5 million chance you'll be bitten by a shark. Yes, you're far more likely to be struck by lightning (1 in 700,000). And there's my personal favorite. You're ten times more likely to be bitten by another human in New York City than you are by a shark anywhere on the planet. I once read that more people are killed by soda machines -- lose your quarter, shake the machine, get crushed -- than sharks, but I could never find the article again, or anything to corroborate it. Still, I approach soda machines warily. Sharks may be every swimmer's worst fear, but you'd be better served looking over your shoulder for crocodiles, who kill about 1,000 of us every year.

But sharks do attack. The oceanic whitetip, which oceanographer Jacques Cousteau once described as "the most dangerous of all sharks," has been known to target shipwreck and plane crash survivors. I personally know a man who was attacked by a white shark (he survived), and I keep an ever-fattening file filled with clippings documenting shark attacks. Again, most victims survive. But some do not. The roots of our shark rapture run deep, soundly anchored in the straightforward abhorrence of being eaten alive.

"We're not just afraid of predators," wrote Harvard sociobiologist Edward O. Wilson. "We're transfixed by them…"

Jaws had a field day with this.

And shark attacks are increasing. The reason is simple. There are more of us in the water. Seven billion and counting.

Oh. The man I knew who was attacked by the white shark?

It happened at Isla Guadalupe.

I don't tell Groth this. I'm sure he already knows.

He doesn't tell us either.

Cage diving is quite safe. First, there are the aforementioned cages. It's true, on rare occasions a smaller juvenile white shark has wormed its way into the cage (there are larger openings in the cages for cameras) and then there's substantial excitement.

"The young ones are unpredictable," says Groth. "They've come through one side and out the other. Eventually."

Other than that, there is no cause for alarm. There's not even scuba gear. Down in the cages we breathe air pumped to us through long lines called hookahs. Groth has hosted clients ages 9 to ninety, from school teachers to London cabbies. Viewing white sharks from a cage requires no specialized skills other than remembering to breathe, which isn't always easy. If possible, Groth and crew like to put newcomers to the ocean in the cages before the sharks show up.

"We like them to practice breathing before we throw five or six apex predators into the mix," says Groth.

Over the three days of our visit, the sharks appear again and again. Sometimes just one. Sometimes three or four.

They seem curious.

Groth believes they are.

"They know what they cages are," he says. "Sometimes they like looking at the monkeys."

Whether this is true or not, it certainly works to our advantage. Often the sharks pass so close to the cage that we can see the intricate beauty of their markings: the ragged line separating their gray forms from their white undersides like a string of low storm clouds. Their languid movements, they drift more than swim, induce a sort of dreamy hypnosis, until they rise to the surface and the crew men, either surprised or generous, allow them a tuna head. Then serenity explodes in a blink-and-you-miss-it devouring. Watching from the safety of the cage I find the convulsive, serrated wrenching not terrifying but moving, for it is a display of primal power and thoughtless efficiency as inspiring as it is rarely seen.

It is something alongside us, and beyond us.

As Alex puts it, "If I see shark, what is time?"

Alex and I share the same feeling of child-like wonder and joy, although Alex is more exuberant.

Emerging from a cage, he performs yet another jig on the stern deck.

"Wooooooo! My dream come true!" he shouts, waving his arms over his head. Dropping his arms, he grins at me. "First question. Who is looking at who? People at shark, or shark at people?"

It is hypnotic. A Groth customer once stayed in the water for nine-and-a-half hours.

It is also odd, and strictly my own wayward imaginings, but often the sharks seem to make us wait. Perhaps they possess a sense of theater. So it is that we turn inside the cages, looking up, looking down, looking out: looking to make sure none of our body parts are poking out of the cage. Collectively we squint into the smoky blue, until suddenly there is an explosion of bubbles and a muffled shout – whose unseemly panic this is, it's impossible to tell – and we bang about inside the cage as a shark passes right off our noses, the eye, tracking us above the signature serrated maw, looking almost amused. Boo.

The visibility is close to 80 feet. Yet they just appear.

When I confide my surprise to crew member Daniel Zapata Lopez, Danny laughs.

"You are looking, looking, looking, and nothing. When you least expect it, they're right in front of your eyes." Laughter gone, Danny holds on to just a fraction of his smile. "This animal is so big and powerful, yet they make no charging noise. They're just on you. That's part of the mystique. They're ambush predators, and we are getting ambushed all day long."

Now you see me, now you don't.

But it is no game.

At night, while we sleep, the sharks feed on the elephant seals. Then they proceed as they wish, as they have done for 600 million years. The perfect survivor, they will almost certainly swim long after mankind is gone.

One afternoon, Danny takes me down in the "cinema cage," so dubbed for the incredible videos divers get. If you are a certified diver, the Solmar V crew will lower you in a cage to a depth of roughly 40 feet. Then, if you are inclined, you can worm through the open hatch and stand on top of the cage with nothing between you and the sharks but blue water. White sharks typically attack from beneath, so the cage, theoretically, still provides protection.

We descend in the cage, Danny and I. The cage comes to a halt. Danny, burbling beside me, peers about. Then he nods and gives me the thumbs up. I worm slowly through the open hatch above our heads. It is true, I do not stand on the roof of the cage immediately. It may even be that I still have half a leg extended down through the hatch. But slowly I extricate that leg, and with equally calculated measure I stand. I swoop my head about like a man working a crick from his neck.

I feel wholly exposed, but the good news is I can see the sharks, who have now appeared, quite clearly. Or at least I see the sharks that deign to be seen. Two big females, they approach from above the cage. As they sweep toward me I feel their menace, but it is my feeling alone. Twenty yards out, collectively they veer away. And so it gloriously goes. They circle back again and again, sunlight rippling along their broad sides as they drop through the water like fat scythes, the loveliest otherworldly ballet. I now stand straight. I have not forgotten my fear. It has simply been usurped by my soaring spirit. It is an intensely powerful moment: like watching the birth of my sons: like standing at the altar looking toward my approaching bride. Danny, sharing the top of the cage with me, turns and gives me a high five.

It sounds overly grand – I am as surprised by the raw upwelling of emotion as anyone -- but it is heartfelt and true.

It is emotion beyond articulation, but I try. That night, after dinner, when I tell Groth how I felt, a softer Lawrence Groth regards me.

"People come here initially looking for a thrill or adventure," he says. "They get that. But allowing them to see the animal as it is in its natural environment, to see how beautiful it is, how graceful it is, how they each have individual personalities, that's the real lesson. So they come away with respect instead of fear. Appreciation instead of ignorance. They see how the sharks really are."

Later that night, I find Alex curled up on a couch in the main cabin.

We have just ingested a dinner of baked chicken. Sharks are not the only predators.

Alex regards me contently, then makes the faintest flapping motion with his arms.

"I am a sea lion," he says.

Out in the darkness, the white sharks hunt.

WATER FOLK

I have many favorite stories regarding the practical outlook of folks who make a life around the water. Here's one.

On the small island of Ocracoke, North Carolina there once lived a man named Cleveland Gaskins: Cle to his friends. Cle once took an interest in some toilet paper he saw advertised in a Sears, Roebuck catalog. This was some time ago, before the point and click age. Having decided to purchase this toilet paper, Cle had his daughter pen a brief letter. "Dear Sears, Roebuck. I would like to buy a dozen rolls of toilet paper. Please send the toilet paper to my home on Ocracoke. Sincerely, Cleveland Gaskins." Cle put the note and the money in an envelope and off it went on the mail boat. Time passed and no toilet paper came. But a letter from Sears, Roebuck did arrive. "Dear Mr. Gaskins. We don't sell toilet paper by the dozen. Please consult our catalog for the quantities we offer." Cle instructed his daughter to craft a response. "Dear Sears, Roebuck. I recently ordered a dozen rolls of toilet paper. Instead I got a letter telling me to order directly from the catalog. Gentlemen, I can assure you, if I had one of your catalogs, I wouldn't need your damn toilet paper."

Cleveland Gaskins couldn't read or write, but he possessed clarity, one of the many traits I admire in water folk. Spinners of (possibly) tall tales, doers of oddball deeds, doers of whatever the hell they want. Tough cusses. Wise and hardened, but not completely. Sometimes criminal, sometimes honest far past a fault: though, in either case, they don't particularly see it that way. Like Cleveland Gaskins, many of the water folk I've known see clearly where they walk. Maybe the things they weather make them different. But often they see through life's mirrors.

I have had the good fortune to spend much of my life around the water, and so I have come to know an assortment of water folk. I am grateful for this. As we walk through life we meet many people. Some are forgettable and some are not, and if you are wise (a qualification I do not always meet) you pay attention to both parties and, when you see the opportunity, you take a piece of them with you. Lessons, maybe. Some are so simple they don't seem lessons at all. But often it's the simple lessons we miss.

The water folk I've known, they have wielded practicality with a subtle wand. Take George Baker. By trade, George, who resides on St. Simons Island in the good state of Georgia, operates a salvage business of sorts, donning dive gear to recover everything from bodies to false teeth from the dark waters of the marshes that clasp his island home. There is substantial sadness in this. Stung by jellyfish, accompanied by water moccasins, George has painstakingly searched midnight dark waters (his business card reads "Blackwater Recovery" with good reason) to find what the family needs. "My expertise is finding victims for their family's sake and, later, for their peace of mind," he says.

But like most water folk, George prefers entertainment to sadness. Which is why he told me this story.

"Got a call once from a visiting tourist, a gentleman who lost his gold and diamond Rolex watch in the water that afternoon," said George. "Boy, was he excited. Turned out, the watch was an anniversary gift from his wife. He told me where he'd lost it, and I told him not to worry. Guaranteed I'd find it for him, and that calmed him a little." In fine storytelling fashion, George took a casual moment to re-gnaw the nub of his cigar. "What he didn't know is the tides in these marshes can be pretty impressive. The difference between high tide and low tide might be six to ten feet. So 'bout three o'clock that morning when the tide had gone out, I sobered up, got my metal detector and my rake…"

Water folk are not inclined to trends. Once I stood beside two fishermen in the town of Murrells Inlet, South Carolina. One man was trying to quit smoking. The other man smoked beside him.

"How ya' doin' with the quittin' smokin'?" the smoking fisherman asked, handing the quitter a cigarette.

The quitter took the cigarette, tapping it in his hand.

"Heard today's the Great American Smokeout," he said.

The two men smoked and considered this fact.

Water folk, their hearts are bushel basket big. When I passed through Murrells Inlet, I was traveling on a finite budget. I'd eaten nothing but soup, soupy offshoots (Ramen noodles), and McDonald's dollar menu items for several weeks. I visited a friend at the H&C Fish Packing House, where I spent several stomach-gnawing hours watching pink slabs of just-off-the-boat fish being boxed for commercial sale. Inside the packing house, the fishermen who had caught the fish came and went, each keeping tabs on their catch and their financial prospects. The packing house was a busy place, filled with the serious business of making a living, and the fishermen paid little attention to a stranger who might have stared a trifle too long at the conveyor belt of fish.

Staring isn't eating. Eventually I walked outside. At the back of the packing house a fisherman I'd seen inside stood with another fisherman, lamenting his busted trip. He'd caught almost nothing, certainly not enough to cover his expenses or the cost of repairing his broken-down boat, which had been towed back to the docks on which he now stood, contemplating his dismal day.

The man held a plastic bag heavy with meaty slabs of filleted grouper. He had a white scar across his brow.

He turned on me suddenly, and the scar cinched down low. I did not pretend to think he didn't know I had been eavesdropping.

"I'm sorry about your troubles," I said, and I genuinely was.

He stood silent, studying me closely. Water folk have a highly refined bullshit-o-meter, probably because they tell their share, and possibly more, of lies. In the eyes below the scar I could see his at work.

"Saw you inside," he said. "Packed this up."

It was my turn to be silent. I had no idea what he meant.

He held the plastic bag out to me.

"Here you go, friend. Fresh fish for dinner."

There are good people everywhere. They are not confined to water. But it is my opinion that water molds folk of generosity and kindness, though it is wise, too, not to mistake kindness for a weak spine. On the Outer Banks of North Carolina I heard the story of a fisherman who had inherited some stock. He wanted to cash it in and buy land and a dock, so he called the broker.

Sell the stock, please, he said, and send me the cash.

You'd be crazy to sell, the broker said. It's gold stock. It'll only go up.

I want to sell.

I can't let you do that.

How about this? Sell it, or I'll come over and shoot you.

"He would have done it too," the storyteller told me.

Water folk, they roll with the changes. In Florida I met Don George. Don was many things in his life, but when I met him, he was laboring hard on behalf of sea turtles. In many places sea turtles are endangered or sorely set upon or both, and Florida is one of them. Don, a biologist by book education, would patrol the beaches near his Cocoa Beach home at dawn, searching for turtle nests, taping them off for protection, meticulously monitoring the nests he had already found. Along the beaches of Patrick Air Force Base and Cape Canaveral, he was the sole line of defense for these prehistoric creatures. He wore turtle T-shirts. He sported a turtle earring. The license plate on his truck read TDL MON.

One evening over dinner, I asked Don if he was attached to sea turtles.

Forking up a chunk of fried fish, he said, "Nope. Ever eaten turtle?"

"No."

"When I was commercial fishing, we'd catch turtle, cut them up into medallions, toss in flour with egg and cream, and pan-fry them. Bites of turtle meat. It's killer."

He rolled his eyes at the memory.

I had spent several days talking with Don about his conservation efforts. Sometime, presented with things that don't seem to make sense, we simply repeat ourselves.

"Why did you eat them?" I asked, though Don had just explained exactly that.

"Back then they weren't endangered," he said.

Water folk are observers, practitioners of stillness in a world that often stampedes sightlessly on. On Long Island in the Bahamas, I walked into Allen Dixon's Everglades Souvenir Shop. Allen wasn't there, no one was, but in my defense the door was open, and from inside the shop phantasmagoric creations – enormous crabs, conch lamps, mirror frames sprouting colorful flowers, a complete bar: each made entirely out of shells - beckoned. I spent the better part of an hour admiring Allen's work and fastidious attention to detail, and when he finally finished his dinner and walked through the door, he simply smiled at me as if we'd spent that hour engaged in amiable conversation.

We engaged in amiable conversation. I learned that Allen Dixon was a clergyman and a studier of driftwood, a man who could make 150 different kinds of flowers out of seashells, but could not tell me how long it took him to make his five-foot-long, waist-high bar completely out of shells.

"I am not exactly sure," he said politely, but what he really meant, I knew, was *Does it matter?*

Many days Allen Dixon walked fifteen miles along the beach gathering material, but he allowed he spent a fair time admiring how light falls upon blue water.

Allen scratched his goatee.

"It is amazing how many people just step past things without seeing them," he said.

Water folk, I have observed, don't miss the moment, perhaps because they know the moment is fleeting. No, they are not always reading to kindergarteners or engaging in Zen contemplations of Bahamian blue. Sometimes they are drinking. Sometimes they are drugging. But whatever they are engaged in, they are wholly engaged. They rarely traffic in distraction.

Perhaps this is because many water folk have had experiences most of us never rub up against, and so they see the world differently. Perhaps they see life's fragility. This is understandable. Often their work pits them against things that would just as soon cripple, ruin or kill them, as give a damn. Nature is like that. Commercial fishing has one of the highest (often it's the highest) fatality rates of any occupation: at times, nine times the rate of firefighters and police. Boats sink in storms, fires burn boats to the waterline, and freighters run them down. Fishermen ignore, or can't afford, safety equipment. Some simply slip and fall overboard in the middle of the night. It is a slow, lonely way to go.

And those are the dangers you might consider.

In Murrells Inlet, I met a gentleman named Harry Strayer. Harry *was* a gentleman. Each morning he welcomed me, and any of the local fishermen, to his trailer for coffee and idle talk. The fishermen came by Harry's trailer even when Harry was out fishing. They just helped themselves.

One morning, sprawled on a couch beneath a poster that read "Beer. Helping Ugly People Have Sex Since 1862" (for water folk are poets too), Harry recounted an experience he'd had one night at sea. While Harry had a flair for the dramatic, he, too, recounted this particular tale in the matter-of-fact manner you might use to describe a toe stubbing while walking your Pekinese. In the early 1970s,

Harry was fishing out of Jacksonville, Florida with a friend who was a retired cop. The friend woke Harry in the middle of the night, waving a pistol in his face, shouting about being boarded.

"He was all kinds of excited," Harry said. "I'm going, 'Now chill out.' Back then I carried this sawed-off shotgun on board. I'd tell people it was for the sharks, but it had other uses. He's radioing the Coast Guard, shouting to them about us being boarded, and giving them our coordinates. I went out on the deck. I could see this other boat. All the lights were off but one, and I could see them lowering a boat off the stern. You could barely hear their motor. My friend is still radioing the Coast Guard, and I'm saying to him, 'No one's crossing this water in front of a sawed-off shotgun.' But looking back on it, it's a good thing he got on the radio because they didn't come across, and that may have been what scared them off."

Harry sipped his coffee.

I worked to piece this together, without luck.

"What were they doing?" I asked.

Harry watched cigarette smoke spiral past his beer poster.

"Well that night, I was guessing it was one of two things," he said. "They were coming for help, or they were coming for my boat. The Coast Guard caught 'em the next day. I walked into a mini-mart, and there's a picture on the front page of the newspaper of that same goddamn boat right there. I mean it stopped me dead in my tracks. That boat was full of pot. Full."

"What would have happened to you?"

Harry stubbed out his cigarette.

"They come on board, slit your stomach open, and throw you overboard, and you're fish food. They use your boat to run the drugs ashore, and then they sink it. Nobody ever knows what happened to you."

Sometimes there isn't a happy ending. Many water folk have known terrible hardship and worse sadness. Perhaps this bestows perspective, but if it does, it is a tough way to get bestowed. I met a man on Tangier Island in the Chesapeake Bay whose brother had drowned while fishing, the drowning of his brother made all the more painful for the man being right alongside him when it happened.

"February 12, 1968," the man said. "Twenty minutes after three."

This man, too, recounted the story matter-of-factly, but he spoke very slowly, as if trying each word on for size. He and his brother were dredging for crabs off Cape Charles, near the mouth of the Chesapeake Bay. They had made their last bottom drag, the dredge rising up out of the water, spilling frigid mud, water and eelgrass. The air was in the mid-twenties. The deck was icy. When both men reached out to grab the chain to pull the dredge in, their collective weight sent them and the dredge back in the water.

The men surfaced within feet of each other. The boat was still in gear. It moved methodically away from them, the chain attached to the dredge spooling out. There were other boats nearby: other crabbers making their own drags. One was fifty feet away. The brothers shouted but no one heard them. The engines churned, and a chill wind blew out of the southwest.

The one brother turned to the other.

Don't they see us?

Nope.

Boy, this is somethin'.

When at last the length of chain played out, roughly 230 feet of it, it brought the boat to a standstill, the dredge in the water acting as an anchor. The boat, now working vainly against the weight of the dredge, began kicking up a foamy froth off the stern. The other crabbers saw this and knew something was wrong.

By now, one brother was frantically trying to hold the other above the water. The shock of the cold, their clothes, the brother's dead weight pulling him down, it was almost too much.

Quick as men can move, the nearest boat was on them. A hand reached down and grabbed the hood of the one brother's sweatshirt.

No, he said. Get my brother.

He was yanked aboard. So was his brother. These days, at any moment, he will still see his brother laying on the engine box, watching him, as the boat rushed for shore. The rest was foggy. The background crackle of the radio, the terse transmissions, an ambulance waiting, a press of hands and faces in the emergency room.

A doctor spoke to him.

You're a lucky man that you didn't drown with your brother.

When the man finished the story, neither of us said anything.

As my friend, shrimper Hunter Forsyth once said, "People dwell on too much about what they don't have instead of being thankful for what they do have."

And then Hunter walked from the water's edge to his brick home and sat down at the piano, the chords drifting out through the screen door into the gloaming evening.

If you love the water, more doors to our watery world ...

OFF SEASON: DISCOVERING AMERICA ON WINTER'S SHORE (non-fiction)
Barnes & Noble Great New Writers award winner

A stone's throw downriver, three shrimp boats rested against the river bank. The name of the nearest boat – Blessed Assurance – was visible across the stern.

Life, of course, is anything but assured. Yet in the very face of this bleak thought, I felt the surge of optimism and hope I feel every time I look on water. Ocean, lake, or river, its prairie spread always leaves me feeling both inconsequential and reassured. Towns, cultures, individual lives and fortunes will flare and fall, but the waters remain, their backdrop of comforting sameness trumpeting continuity and, with that continuity, hope. Like children, we need something to believe in, a face that will always be there, an anchor we can always return to, and when we can't return, our children can, and their children too.

ISLANDS APART: A YEAR ON THE EDGE OF CIVILIZATION (non-fiction)
"Careful, poetic and often funny... A rumination on what it means to be human." Virtuoso Life Magazine

Most of the elephant seals and sea lions were down near the water's edge, and the longer I watched them, the more they assumed human characteristics. The male elephant seals made their slow rippling way through the crowd like distinguished gendarmes. The juvenile sea lions swaggered along the water's edge like strutting teens. And – my personal favorite - out in the waves the dark forms of small pups played as if no one was watching. For a time I amused myself by watching a female elephant seal rebuff the advances of a mildly amorous male. Inch-worming close, he would drape an enormous proprietary flipper over her. In response she would use her own flippers to douse him with sand before moving away. This repeated itself at least a half dozen times. Oddly, I recalled several of my own early courtships. It was a beach scene reminiscent of the Jersey Shore or Coney Island; a mass of life swaying to nature's urges. Of course pinnipeds are nothing like us, but the thought was entertaining and I am easily amused.

FOG (fiction)
"A 21st century Moby Dick." Richard Boonisar, Cape Cod maritime historian

Cole stood at the edge of the cliffs, considering the dark water. One mistake—a boat turned broadside, a misstep among coiled lines, a back turned to a panicked sailor—and water's caress would provide ablution. Those very mistakes, and hundreds of feckless permutations, killed men regularly. Sometimes in the middle of a rescue, while the steering oar wrenched like a terrified animal in his hands, he would absorb the unfolding carnage with detached curiosity. The black heavens, the leaping waves like wildly snatching hands, the surfboat angling dangerously, the men pulling frantically at the oars, all of it became a siren call. How easy to lean, to slip overboard, a moment's discomfort as the body reflexively fought to save itself, and then nothing.

But then he would return to nature's yowl and see the strained faces of the men, their eyes fixed on him while they put their fear into the oar. He was their shepherd in a cathedral turned inside out and screaming. He could not walk away.

TOGETHER WE JUMP (fiction)
"There's a beautiful Forrest Gump feel to the book. The main character was a delight and I just loved his sad, wistful, wonderful tale." Ann Oldenburg, USA Today

My drowsy inebriation vanished. I waited, hoping for a redirection, a turtle banking in the deeps. *La esperanza muere al ultimo.* Hope is the last thing to die.
"What happened?" Abby said softly.

"To what?" I asked, though I knew.

"To the boy who swam with turtles. To the man I thought I married. To the truth."

There are moments when you can save yourself, when the right word, the honest confession, can turn you back on to the road to redemption. Sometimes you even see these moments as they arrive. But you can read these words and know they are true, just as you can see these moments in your own life and still ignore them. Just as you will see, as the years pass, and you grow old, how you will relive these moments again and again, returned to like carrion to something never quite dead. Regret is the sharpest thorn.

JUNCTURE (fiction)
"A cerebral Jaws."

Surrounded by forest, the dark green marine lake might have been a lake of her childhood dreams. Across the lake she saw dangling vines and explosions of hibiscus. And there was no one else, this communion with Nature hers alone. Sitting on the end of the dock, she slipped on fins and mask. Settling the snorkel firmly in her mouth, she pushed up with her hands and plunged forward into the lake.

Halfway across the lake, all familiarity disappeared. The first jellyfish were scattered individuals, opaque softballs pulsing in the murk. So beautiful, their pulsing like a serene heartbeat. As she finned forward, their numbers grew. Within a minute, the water was a gelatinous cloud. The massing of the jellyfish, some now the size of cantaloupes, might have given someone else pause, but she had read everything there was to read about the lake, and she knew that even the largest jellyfish possessed only enough sting to prey on shrimp-like copepods. At most she would feel a mild itching, perhaps here and there the faintest kiss of sting. The silky brush of dozens of jellyfish was erotic, like hands everywhere, the multiple lovers she had never had.

It was erotic, divine and beautiful, and then it was not.

WEST IS EDEN: REFLECTIONS ON THIS GIFT CALLED LIFE
(Life Essays)

My friend Bill Bones had a simple way of quantifying a wave's value for visiting surfers. By visiting surfers I mean surfers who didn't live in our New Jersey beach town. How many teeth might the ride be worth? Bones was twenty years older than the rest of us, but he was also fit, large and very quick. He didn't pummel every visitor who paddled out, that would have interfered with his opportunity to catch waves, but he made it clear that he might. His size, coupled with a propensity for sudden irrational behavior, kept the best waves at our local break largely to us, with visitors picking up the scraps. I am not saying I condone such behavior. I am just reporting how it was. Bones put a concrete value on waves, and visitors decided if their dental insurance was up to it or not.

LIGHTNING STRIKES OF LOOPY GIDDINESS AND OTHER BUCKET LIST TRAVEL TALES (Travel essays taken from 25 years of magazine travel writing)

We see it first in the distance, far out to sea, far as a child's eyes can see from the shore of this desolate island off the west coast of Malaysia, a thin thread, upright, moving toward shore like a loopy periscope. The periscope bends and sways as if passing through its own private breezes. I stand on the beach, one in a knot of walnut-brown kids, the lot of us squinting, shouting and hopping up and down in an attempt to get a better look at this oscillating mirage floating across a vast plain of sea blasted by equatorial sunshine.

Behind us there is jungle. Along the beach, palms and pines click and whisper, and an occasional monkey screams. The undulating periscope, proceeding toward us, teases us. We cannot quite see. It seems to neither gain distance nor lose it, like some galloping horseman forever pinned to the horizon. Of course the featureless sea only makes this seem so. Soon enough an older boy among us whispers, "Cobra."

Ken McAlpine is the author of eight other books: a collection of fiction, non-fiction and essays. He lives in Ventura, California with his wife and two sons.

For more on Ken's books, please see www.kenmcalpine.com.

You can visit Ken on facebook at
www.facebook.com/kenmcalpineauthor

Thank you for your interest.